E PLURIBUS
KINKO'S

A Story of Business, Democracy,
and Freaky Smart People

By Dean Zatkowsky
Foreword by Paul Orfalea

Notice

Although the author has made every effort to ensure the accuracy and completeness of information contained in this book, we assume no responsibility for errors, inaccuracies, omissions, or any inconsistencies herein. In offering our opinions on leadership, management, and business in general, we intend no harm or offense to any individual or organization and hope none is taken. All trademarks used are the property of their respective owners.

© 2009 Dizzy One Ventures LLC
All Rights Reserved
ISBN: 1-4392-5507-5
ISBN-13: 9781439255070
LCCN: 2009908579
Visit www.booksurge.com to order additional copies.

Table of Contents

News Item: June 6, 2008 v
Foreword: Culture Comes from People, not Policies vii
Prologue: Fall 1999 xi

SECTION 1:
BOY MEETS BUSINESS 1

Inexperienced, Unqualified, and Hired! 3
The State of the Union 1986 7
Come As You Are 13
Theory X & Theory Why 17
Take Me to Your Leaders 23
Foundations of Democracy 37
Kamelot? 41

SECTION 2:
BOY AND BUSINESS TAKE A VOW 49

The Kinko's Philosophy 51
"It's Like The Constitution" 55
A Living Document 85
Unambiguously Paradoxical 89

SECTION 3:
BOY AND BUSINESS GROW TOGETHER 91

Limited Partnerships of Unlimited Potential 93
A Wide Range of Talent and Ability 99
Profit-Sharing 103
Ambassadors of Capitalism 111
Controlling Costs Without Cutting Corners 115
Ripples of Prosperity 119
Lowering The Bottom Line 123
Compensation Alone Does Not Create Engagement ... 127
Participation 129

SECTION 4:
BOY AND BUSINESS QUARREL 157

Attention Deficit Dynamic 159
Public Conflict in a Private Company 165
The Power Pendulum 173
Permutations & Pluralism—In Ideas We Trust 179
Playfulness 187
"…But Now You Stop and Think About Your Dignity" ... 193

EPILOGUE: BOY GETS DUMPED 195

Those Who Learn from the Past 197
What Makes You So Special? 207

AFTERWORD: BRAD AND STUIE 211

APPENDIX: 213

10 SUGGESTIONS FOR A HEALTHY
COMMERCIAL DEMOCRACY 215

ACKNOWLEDGEMENTS 219

ABOUT THE AUTHOR 220

News Item: June 6, 2008

MEMPHIS (AP) — FedEx said Monday it plans to stop using the Kinko's name on its copy and office service stores and book an $891 million charge for the quarter that ended Saturday.

The charge relates to a decision about the use of the Kinko's name and a write-down of the value of its acquisition of the brand. The charge, which works out to $2.22 a share, was not part of FedEx's earnings forecast. The company reports its financial results for the fiscal fourth quarter June 18.

FedEx (FDX) said it will change the name of its FedEx Kinko's stores to FedEx Office over the next several years.

"The FedEx Office name better describes the wide range of services available at its retail centers and takes full advantage of the FedEx brand long recognized for excellent customer service, quality, and reliability," spokesman Jess Bunn said.

Foreword: Culture Comes from People, not Policies

By Paul J. Orfalea, Founder, Kinko's

The term "company culture" can mean a lot of different things. In the worst of environments, the expression might be code for racism or sexism. In the best of environments, company culture reflects high-minded ideals that appeal to—and inspire—coworkers, customers, vendors, and communities. While growing Kinko's from a single shop to a $2 billion industry leader, we tried to maintain a very democratic company culture, understanding that our customers, coworkers, vendors, and the larger community were all the same people.

Misunderstanding a market can cost a company some money. Misunderstanding your own culture can cost a lot more, and that is what derails a lot of mergers and acquisitions. Viewing the entire range of stakeholders as part of our culture allowed our leaders to obsess over the company culture without becoming excessively inward-focused.

E Pluribus Kinko's

Here's one example of the value of inclusive, rather than inward, focus:

In the mid-1980s, Kinko's advertised that we offered copies, binding, and passport photos. Every ad promoted the fact that we were open early, open late, and open weekends. Our extended hours constituted a competitive advantage over the quick-print shops offering similar services.

Then, a handful of stores in Chicago got so busy that they asked some of their Key Operators (the most highly trained production experts, also known as Copy Jocks or Copy Gods) to work graveyard shifts. The Key Ops reported that people occasionally tapped on the windows to see if the store was open. We decided to unlock the doors.

This did not noticeably spike sales, but we heard from a convenience store owner that we would see an improvement in daytime sales if we stayed open at night. So we advertised that the stores were open 24 hours. As the convenience store owner predicted, this did not spike graveyard shift sales, *but the daytime business almost doubled.* It didn't take long for most of my partners across the country to adopt this successful practice. Eventually, all Kinko's stores were open 24 hours and it was an essential element of our brand identity.

If you planned to go to Kinko's after work, delays at the office did not create additional stress for you, because you could go to any Kinko's any time. Likewise, you could pick up orders on the way to work. The power of Open 24 Hours was psychological—it positioned Kinko's as a reliable resource, and separated us clearly from other providers of business services. Over the years, *Open 24 Hours became a significant point of pride for our coworkers and a security blanket for our customers.* It was a cultural touchstone.

But anyone with a calculator or spreadsheet could "prove" that being open around the clock was unprofitable. After all, we hardly rang up any sales between midnight and 7:00 AM. When the company's new owners chose to reduce operating hours in most stores, they replaced simplicity and reliability with complexity and uncertainty for customers. And remember: customers are as much a part of company culture as coworkers, especially in a service business.

An owner or chief executive's primary responsibility is company culture. Anyone can see numbers on the P&L, but who takes time to understand, appreciate, and advocate the environment itself? I hope you do. This is the work of leadership.

I've been working with Dean Zatkowsky since 1986 and, while we often disagree about the meaning of specific events in Kinko's past, we share a passionate belief that the company culture was something truly special and a good model for entrepreneurs. As Dean says in this book, there are tens of thousands of perspectives on the Kinko's culture, one for every coworker in the company's history. Dean's focus on the democratic structure expressed through our Philosophy, our Partnership ethos, and our constant Pot-stirring captures the key success factors as well as any analysis I've heard.

Over the years, we sent many Kinko's managers and executives to the Management Action Program (www.mapconsulting.com), a workshop designed to help people build on their personal and professional strengths. Among other things, the workshop requires attendees to face a stark—and often harsh—appraisal of their professional strengths and weaknesses. But rather than dwell on weaknesses, as most people do, the program teaches attendees how to focus more attention on their strengths. Unless they are dangerous, weaknesses are to be ignored or marginalized.

That's what Dean does in this book: he acknowledges our weaknesses, but celebrates our strengths, so others can see how democratic principles made our company stronger, smarter, and more agile (even if we paid a price in frustration and inefficiency).

To all of our coworkers who lived the Philosophy, treated one another as partners, and fearlessly shared controversial ideas, you kept the company innovative and exciting, and we thank you for giving the world a company culture we can still point to with pride.

Prologue: Fall 1999

On a bright, warm Saturday morning in September 1999, I slowly walked down a quiet hallway of the Kinko's headquarters building in Ventura, California. Heading for the exit, I thought it was a pity the automatic lights didn't dim behind me as I carried my box of junk down the hall, the way they automatically lit the path ahead as I entered. Those automatic lights always smacked of the supernatural when I visited the building late at night or on the weekend to finish an ad, or pick up a book, or hang the pirate flag in my office. I'd stroll forward and the lights would flicker to life one-by-one, much as the sidewalk squares lit up for Michael Jackson in the *Billie Jean* video. The lights stayed on for quite a while once they had been triggered, so I questioned the "energy-saving" technology.

I first noticed the paradox of the "energy-saving" automatic lights the night my brother died in June of 1992. After my sister called with the news, my first impulse was to get to the office. I was supposed to moderate a customer focus group in Seattle the next day, so I had to cancel my travel plans, reorganize the week's work, and contact the Puget Sound Regional Manager to run the focus group for me. It only took a few minutes, but I stayed at my desk for half an hour or so, thinking about my brother, who died two months shy of his 42nd birthday, and my new daughter, who was less than a month old.

I stayed still for so long that the lights in the building went out again. I sat in the darkness of my office for a while, because there were few places I felt so comfortable. But I knew my parents would need me, so I got up and walked out, triggering the lights again. A few minutes later, as I drove out of the vast empty parking lot, I felt guilty looking at the brightly lit building, wondering how much energy had been wasted because I stayed too long.

Seven years later, as I carried my belongings down the hall, I was 41 years old, my career was over, and most of my friends and longtime coworkers had already left the company, literally or figuratively. My collection of dirty coffee mugs clinked in the banker's box as I hauled it toward the stairwell—until I stopped suddenly.

I froze midway down the hall, flanked by fuzzy beige cubicle walls. No phones ringing or keyboards tapping. No animated conversations or friendly laughter. No colorful clothes or accents. No scent of microwave popcorn mingling with perfume and aftershave. I rocked on the soft, silent carpet pads under my feet. I knew it was a bright, warm day outside, but the temperature inside the building was so carefully regulated that I felt neither warm nor cold. I smiled. The absence of sights, smells, sounds, and feelings confirmed what I had always preached: without the people, Kinko's was nothing.

Outside, I loaded my books, coffee mugs, and pirate flag into the car. I looked back at the building, the flagpoles, and the fountain. I looked at the trees we planted in memory of deceased coworkers. I looked at the baseball diamond, running track, daycare center, and lemon orchard. Feeling the knot in my throat as I drove past the security gate for the last time, I wondered again how much energy had been wasted because I stayed too long.

For the better part of the next decade, I tried not to think about Kinko's, with varying degrees of success. Then, when I read the announcement that FedEx would be eliminating the Kinko's name, I was flooded with unexpected and very emotional memories of adventures and accomplishments, friends and mentors. I had always expected to tell my future grandchildren that I helped to build Kinko's. I never expected they might respond, "What's a Kinko's?" Stranger still, I got the news while on the road, watching television in a little motel room, just as I had for two or three nights a week when I worked at Kinko's. And I wondered, was it all just a dream? To answer that question, I had to write this book.

SECTION 1: BOY MEETS BUSINESS

Inexperienced, Unqualified, and Hired!

I stared at my tan, hard-shell Samsonite briefcase, wondering how long I'd be in prison if I used it to smash the skull of the woman at the next desk. She was talking to her computer again—moaning and whining really—but it was 1985 and, as I look back, I guess there was a lot to moan about. Still, prison was starting to look pretty good to me. She fretted and jabbered over the machine every day, and each day I would reboot her computer ten or twelve times and try to undo the damage caused by her desperate, arbitrary keyboard flailing. I was twenty-seven and every day at work was another day of rage.

But this day was different. I was exhausted, recovering from a month-long bout of pneumonia, and my mind had pretty much snapped. Instead of killing my coworker, I calmly carried my briefcase out of the office, walked a mile or two from the University of California, Santa Barbara, campus to the airport, boarded a plane for Las Vegas, and spent a couple days drinking beer and losing my meager savings. My wife, though not amused, was remarkably supportive, so I returned home and started looking for a new job.

Like many unemployed southern Californians, I spent a few weeks writing a screenplay. Then I took a job at a used computer brokerage, where I not only sold pre-owned computers, but also learned to build PC clones. This was a great experience, but I was determined to recast myself as a writer, so I applied for a copywriting job at a young, private company called Microsoft. Shockingly, I landed an interview, for which they flew me to Seattle. The interview proved to me—and the interviewer—that I had no idea what copywriting or Microsoft were all about. But what I learned that day made a friend of mine a lot of money in October, 1987, when the stock market crashed, dragging the newly public Microsoft with it. He had just sold a house, so I told him to scoop up as much Microsoft stock as possible.

I was glad to help him, because about eighteen months earlier, he was the one who showed me the ad from the *Santa Barbara News-Press*. Something called KSC was looking for a copywriter. With a little research, I ascertained that the company was Kinko's and, having been a Kinko's customer for several years, I was sure my enthusiasm could more than make up for my lack of experience. Besides, how hard could it be to write ads for a couple of local copy shops?

When I dropped off my first resume package with receptionist Debbie Seymour at the Kinko's Service Corporation (KSC) offices at 4141 State Street, the folly of my effort hit me in the face. Behind her was a map of the United States with about 100 pins in it. Kinko's was a big company; they wouldn't want to hire an inexperienced copywriter.

Kinko's Service Corporation included a Finance Department that handled accounts payable; PSW Financing (a sort of internal bank); a Technology department to help stores with things like phone systems, cash registers, and those new computers arriving in offices and customer areas; an Operations department that handled HR, training, purchasing, and systems, and the Marketing department. Marketing handled yellow page advertising, marketing materials (printed ad slicks, for example), copyright issues, signs/merchandising, national advertising, etc. As a group, KSC also produced and hosted the annual Picnic, a huge gathering of managers, partners, vendors, and staff.

As I said, I dropped off "my first resume package." Before the hiring process was over, I would have to submit three, because Marketing Department Vice President, Charley Williams, kept losing them. Later, coworkers explained that his office was a black hole that seemed to suck up everything except the many coffee rings staining each horizontal surface.

During my first interview, I noticed that Charley's walls were covered with framed letters from prestigious universities and film schools. Later, I was very unfair and unkind to Charley; but I liked him immediately when we met and liked him even more when I read the letters on display and realized they were all rejection letters. Ask anyone married or who has been working with the same person for more than twenty years, and they'll tell you that a sense of humor is the key success factor in the relationship. Even though I would later find Charley impossible to work with, he was—and is—intelligent, funny, friendly, and *cool*. I also concede that he consistently got me to do work of better quality than I imagined I could, although he made me suffer for it.

I had to interview with every coworker in the department and create sample ads for the Professor Publishing program. The process took weeks, but every contact with Kinko's coworkers increased my desire to land the job. Later, I learned to appreciate the value of the team interview in a profit-sharing environment, but at the time it seemed excessive.

During my interview with Marketing Evangelist Adrianna Foss and Graphic Artist Rod Tryon, I couldn't help but notice their nervousness, and being who I am, I couldn't help but comment on it. My candor seemed to put them at ease, and they explained that they were nervous for two reasons. In the first place, they were surprised at being asked to interview applicants and were not prepared. In the second place, they were nervous because a few days earlier, an electrician had fallen through the ceiling tiles onto the table at which we were seated—during a meeting. So that's why their eyes drifted upward at every creak of the building.

It was my first hint that I might be entering a world where anything could happen. The second hint came when Charley offered me the job.

The State of the Union 1986

My first week as a Kinko's coworker set the tone for much of what followed. Beautiful, radiantly intelligent Adrianna Foss conducted my initial orientation. I fell instantly in love. Not a good habit for a married man, but I defy any man to spend a few minutes with Adrianna without falling for her. Besides, one of the great arguments for gender equality in business is the fact that a lot of men behave best when they are trying to impress a woman. Just watch them suck in their guts, literally and figuratively. Working with Adrianna made me want to be brilliant and I'm confident I was not an isolated case.

She explained to me that the Marketing Department was part of Kinko's Service Corporation, recently created to serve the stores. My belief in that ideal—that the corporate office exists to serve the coworkers in the field—contributed to my ouster years later, but throughout my career—at Kinko's and beyond—I have found it a great source of moral strength: To lead is to serve.

The El Mercado Plaza at 4141 State Street in Santa Barbara, California, was designed to house retail shops on the ground floor, with offices above. When I arrived in 1986, there was a Kinko's store at the front, a Mexican restaurant in the back, a dentist's office, and a whole lot of Kinko's offices spread throughout the complex. I would guess we occupied 80% of the square footage, and our offices were getting more cramped every day.

As Adrianna took me on a tour of the maze and introduced me to coworkers in other departments and adjacent partnership offices, everyone we met asked the same wide-eyed question: "Where is he going to sit?" It seemed like a running gag. The organization was outgrowing space as fast as it signed leases, but I couldn't see what all the fuss was about. In fact, these questions made me feel very special, because I had a comfortable workspace. On my first day, Charley showed me to my desk, already equipped with a Macintosh computer (probably a 512k model!), a stack of advertising tear sheets to review, and drawers full of files and office supplies. Obviously, I was important enough that a space had been prepared in advance of my arrival.

It wasn't until the end of the week—when Maggie McMurray returned from a business trip to find me at her desk—that I realized: a) I wasn't as special as I imagined, and b) Charley and the other VPs were making things up as they went along. I spent much of the next two years resenting Charley for his lack of omniscience. Only with age and responsibility did I come to appreciate the load he and the other young managers bore. Karen Parrish, VP of Operations; Ed Togami, VP of Technology; Ross Waddell,

VP of Finance; and Charley Williams, VP of Marketing, were all under thirty, running a company that was growing like crazy but completely dependent on Fall and Spring cash-flow peaks. They were as much *explorers* as managers.

To her credit, Maggie took my usurpation of her space in stride. Now a junior high school science teacher, Maggie is one of those coworkers every manager desires. Thoughtful, dedicated, and persistent, Maggie took on projects without complaint and put her nose to the grindstone until they were successfully accomplished. During my time at KSC, Maggie was responsible for the rollout of fax machines and Kodak floppy diskettes. Later, she fulfilled a variety of roles in the organization, but everything she did, she did well and without self-aggrandizement.

What impressed me most during my first week at Kinko's was the fact that we had three parties. And I don't mean a few coworkers standing around a birthday celebrant eating doughnuts. We got *swacked*. In large numbers. We celebrated the arrival of New Manager Training attendees, celebrated the graduation of New Manager Training attendees, and celebrated the fact that Paul liked the month-end numbers (even though they later turned out to be wrong). I drank more beer in my first week at Kinko's than I had in the previous year and I thought, "Yeah, I can work here."

I also picked up a lot of mythology in those first weeks—tales absurd and probably apocryphal, but intriguing nevertheless. Did a couple of Regional Managers really dump an unconscious Paul Orfalea into a snowdrift in the middle of the night so they could use the back seat of the car for a while? Was it true that most stores kept a stash of pot under their main production machine? At the company Picnic, were bathroom gender designations mere suggestions? Did a manager really disappear into the forests of Humboldt County for a year and then return with enough money to open his own partnership? And of course, tales of five-figure monthly bonus checks circulated freely. The place sounded like fun to me.

Because Kinko's Service Corporation paid bills for most of the stores, we also got their advertising tear sheets, so my first job was to review the ads and critique them for the stores. That is to say, I had to call the stores to suggest that, in the future, they might consider adding the company logo, or their address and phone number, or some reference to their services. Sometimes I could not contact the store, because I could not figure out which store to call: the ad didn't offer a single clue. At the time, it was a free-for-all. Stores could do pretty much anything they liked. For the most part, they did a brilliant job. Besides, we could afford to experiment because the business was ridiculously profitable. Our three main services at the time were copies, binding, and passport photos, and the gross profit was well above 90%. That kind of profit covers a multitude of sins, but frugality is at the heart of Paul Orfalea's entrepreneurial philosophy, so KSC watched for waste.

When it comes to waste, every company looks at advertising first, and rightfully so. Long ago, William Wrigley declared that half of his advertising expenses were wasted, but he didn't know which half. The advertising industry uses its considerable powers of persuasion to convince clients that advertising is a science, but they rig the game by devising their own measurement criteria. And they get paid whether the client profits from their efforts or not. That's why I've always preferred in-house marketing departments aligned to the company's goals.

Advertising was a weak spot for Kinko's, because most people believe advertising is about art and creativity, and exceptionally artistic and creative people staffed our stores. Much of my role was to educate coworkers about goals, strategies, and tactics for *effective* advertising. In 1986, all I had to do was learn about it first.

Come As You Are

A few days after joining the company, as fear of my own ignorance gripped me, I asked Charley why he had hired me, since I had no training or experience in advertising or copywriting. He said he hired for attitude and creativity because "skills can be taught—and, by the way, here's a list of local copywriting seminars." Within a couple of years, it would have been impossible for someone so inexperienced to get hired at KSC; I was in the right place at the right time. And Charley's approach to hiring is, in my opinion, spot on. I preached it for years, when managers asked my advice, and I adopted it as my own policy. I don't believe you should waste time and effort trying to motivate people when you can hire motivated people instead. As Charley understood, it's a lot easier to teach copywriting than to instill values.

During my second week with the company, as I was cleaning out heaps of junk in search of a new place to sit, I found a promotional mailer from Xerox: an oversize direct mail piece that featured 24"x36" copies held together

E Pluribus Kinko's

by a giant chrome paperclip. I took possession of the clip, dubbed it the Giant Paperclip of Doom, and carried it like a walking stick for months, used it as a pointer during presentations, and pretty much kept it in my cubicle or office for the rest of my career. In retrospect, it was a pretty good symbol of the company's tolerance for eccentricities. In fact, within a few months of joining Kinko's, I was telling friends I had found my place in the business world: an organization that not only tolerated my eccentricities, but encouraged them. For example, I never used a laser pointer during my presentations, but over the years, I used a plastic lobster, a dancer's cane, a toy laser saber, and—near the end—a Harry Potter wand. So many workplaces require coworkers to put on masks when they punch the clock, but not Kinko's. In the 1980s and early 1990s, as long as you brought something to the party, it was "come as you are."

By the early eighties, the business was growing in complexity as it grew in number of stores. We started to offer Macintosh computers alongside our typewriters and Kroy lettering machines. Apple introduced the LaserWriter and Adobe introduced PageMaker, creating desktop publishing. Fax machines were common in large companies, but still too expensive for small offices, so we began to offer fax services. To manage this growing complexity and to provide new opportunity for more experienced managers, the position of Regional Manager spread across the partnerships.

Mike Fasth, later President of Kinko's Northwest, was one of the first Regional Managers. As a store manager, he had to figure out EVERYTHING for himself, so he viewed the position of Regional Manager as a mentor function.

The early Regional Managers were predominantly regional trainers who hired managers and taught them how to run the stores. The Regional Manager held P&L responsibility for large swaths of business, handling everything from real estate to machine contracts to human resources to training to new product development to litigation. Over the years, I met a lot of exceptional people at every level of the Kinko's organization. To this day I believe a random sample of five Kinko's Regional Managers from that era could have gotten together and fixed any troubled business in America, from General Motors on down.

The Coworker's Voice

In early December 1981, I was 28 years old and had recently relocated to New Orleans from a secure laboratory job at the University of Kansas, pursuing a dream to play in my sister's rock and roll band. My prospects for a day job were limited, with unemployment in double digits and an oil bust that had hit New Orleans particularly hard.

My sister recommended that I try applying at Kinko's where we got our band flyers (and my résumés) copied. She reminded me that the lady there seemed pretty cool (and cute). I took my sister's advice and set up an appointment with manager Annie Groves. I arrived promptly at 1:00 PM and, after a brief wait, Annie ushered me into a small office, where her German Shepherd, C'mere, lying calmly next to her desk, greeted me. We had a pleasant interview, where I was gently informed that I was overdressed (tweed jacket and tie) and probably overqualified, given my degree in cell biology. Between puffs on her cigarette, Annie asked if I would mind working

E Pluribus Kinko's

at the new downtown location. I left the interview wondering if I had gotten the job (at a whopping $3.85 per hour.)

I worked downtown for a year, commuting to work on the St. Charles streetcar line. Most of my contact with Annie during that period was by phone. She called regularly for sales information and was thrilled at our first $500 day. One day in May 1982, New Orleans was flooded. I called Annie to tell her that I could not get out of my house due to flooding. Undaunted, and probably assuming I was just another slacker, she kindly offered to drive me to work that day. I waded through 3 blocks of hip deep water, with a pair of dry pants and a shirt held high over my head, and met her on St. Charles Avenue. Although mildly irritated, I thought nothing of it; it was just the way we did business at Kinko's. Annie taught me that the glass is always half full; you just have to make the best of any situation. We didn't have a $500 day that day, but we did have a number of amazed and grateful customers.

After about a-year-and–a-half, I was deemed experienced enough to be the "interim" store manager, and a couple of months later, a "real" store manager. By 1983, Annie and I were dating. We married in 1985, had four children, and are still happily married.

—John Odell, Regional Manager, Southeast Kinko's

Theory X & Theory Why

There are many ways to run a company and achieve success, and no one knows if Kinko's key success factors will work for any other company. I want to tell you what I saw and why I believe it's important. Lots of business books tell you that you must execute their entire list of recommendations or all bets are off. Isn't that a convenient way to evade accountability? All bets are always off when it comes to business advice, because no two companies are the same, and no two companies operate under the same conditions. As Heraclites observed, "You can never step in the same river twice." Your situation is unique, and whether and how you choose to analyze and adopt the methods that worked for Kinko's is up to you. I'm just explaining how and why I think it worked for us.

But first, think about the world in 1960, ten years before Paul Orfalea opened the first Kinko's in Isla Vista, California. In 1960, Senator John Kennedy was running for President, the Beatles were playing small clubs in

Liverpool and Hamburg, men wore suits and hats when going for a walk in the park, Europe and Japan were still recovering from the devastation of World War II, and the United States was the international center of finance, industry, and manufacturing. But despite America's rising wealth and experience, business management theories in 1960 were little different from those of 1930 or 1890.

Then, Douglas McGregor of the MIT Sloan School of Management wrote *The Human Side of Enterprise* (McGraw-Hill, 1960), in which he asked leaders to reconsider their beliefs about human resource management. McGregor codified what exceptional leaders like David Packard and Bill Hewlett had already discovered independently—that people respond differently to different types of motivation, depending on each individual's personal needs.

Using Abraham Maslow's hierarchy of needs as a point of departure, McGregor described Theory X and Theory Y models of management. Theory X had been the dominant model up to that time, and it assumed that human beings inherently dislike work and seek to avoid it. Under this model, people must be guided, coerced, or controlled by management, sometimes through threats. According to Theory X, people work only for money and security. Since Theory X assumes that people dislike responsibility and want to be directed, there is no ill will in management's establishment of highly structured, top-down hierarchies. Such structures seem the only logical way to achieve organizational goals.

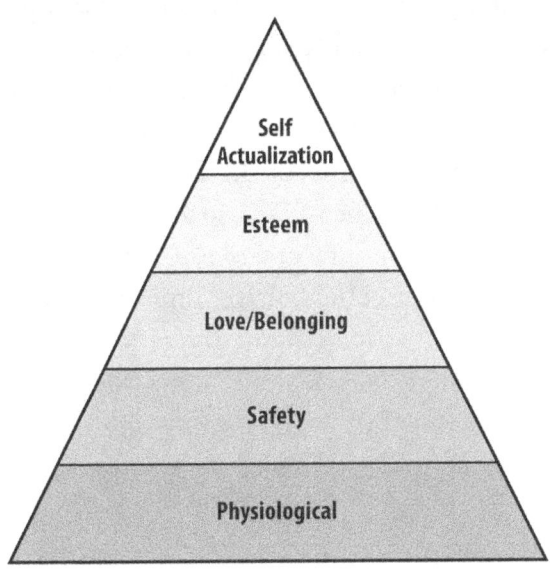

Maslow's Hierarchy of Needs

Abraham Maslow's study of human motivation led to his 1943 publication of this chart, which illustrates that higher level needs are aroused once more basic needs are met.

McGregor recognized that under Theory X, workers would actually lose motivation as their base-level needs for money and security were met, since organizations managing via Theory X would offer no higher-level satisfaction, such as feelings of belonging, esteem, or self-actualization—the upper levels of Maslow's hierarchy.

Theory Y builds on different assumptions and offers a management style more appropriate for knowledge workers, service workers, professionals, and managers.

Theory Y assumes that people view work as natural and desirable, learn to accept and seek responsibility, and will eagerly work toward the aims of the organization if their own interests are aligned. Theory Y also assumes that people are naturally imaginative and creative. Companies employing Theory Y tend to be collaborative, innovative workplaces.

	Theory X	**Theory Y**
ASSUMPTIONS	Humans dislike work and avoid it when possible.	People view work as a natural part of their lives.
	Average employees desire direction.	Motivated people direct themselves to the goals of the organization.
	People avoid responsibility.	People learn to accept and seek responsibility.
	People are insecure and need the security of a structured work environment.	People are naturally creative and can flourish in a less structured, problem-solving environment.
APPLICATION	Production workers in large-scale, efficiency-driven organizations such as mass manufacturing.	Professional services, knowledge workers and managers in organizations requiring complex problem solving.
MANAGEMENT STYLE	Authoritarian	Collaborative

Theory X and Theory Y Management

Douglas McGregor felt that Theory Y was a preferable approach to management, but he conceded it was difficult to use in large-scale organizations. A democratic company leans toward Theory Y, but, ironically, requires very strong leadership to keep people engaged.

At first glance, Theory Y seems automatically superior to Theory X, but nothing involving humans is ever that simple. We all know workers who fit the assumptions of Theory X; some people really do lack self-motivation and respond only to external stimuli. Also, many types of work require less collaborative management styles. For example, we expect an army unit or a nuclear power plant to rely on strict adherence to established protocol.

One job of management is optimal application of resources, whether financial, mechanical, or human. The more one studies Theory X and Theory Y, the more comfortable one becomes with Theory WHY, seeking the best fit of management style and business unit.

The important question is not which approach a company uses, but why and how. Of course, that also depends on whom. Over the years, Kinko's benefitted from a collective of talented partners and coworkers, but two men who loomed large during the golden years of growth and profitability serve as excellent symbols of the messy democracy that made the company so successful: Kinko's Founder, Paul Orfalea, and Kinko's Service Corporation President, Dan Frederickson.

Take Me to Your Leaders

I felt like an alien when I joined Kinko's in 1986. As a coworker at the national "Kinko's Service Corporation" (KSC) who had not begun my career in a store or some other "operations" capacity, I required a crash course in company history and culture. Here's yours:

Paul Orfalea founded Kinko's in 1970 with a small loan co-signed by his father. He set up shop in a 100-square-foot space annexed to a hamburger joint near the campus of the University of California Santa Barbara (UCSB). He sold Xerox and Kodak copies, film processing, pens, and notebooks. Thirty years later, Paul left Kinko's when the company boasted 1,000 stores and was doing about $2 billion in sales.

Now, I know there are plenty of success stories in American business. As Paul often tells audiences, just open up the yellow pages if you want to read success stories. But Kinko's was different, not least because we became a $2 billion

E Pluribus Kinko's

company selling a five-cent product, before the Internet made high-volume, low-price businesses so common.

Two big ideas gave Kinko's a huge competitive advantage in the early years: the limited partnership ownership structure and a product called Professor Publishing. The partnership structure sped growth as people invested their own money and sweat equity to open stores, and it also bound the partners to each other through financial exposure—they sank or swam together.

If you went to college in the 1980s, odds are pretty good you bought course packets from Kinko's. Instructors supplied the original materials to us. We copied and bound the packets, and then sold them directly to the students. For the students, this was a convenient alternative to the reserved book room of the library and an inexpensive alternative to obscenely overpriced textbooks. For professors, course packets allowed use of a broader and custom-tailored range of book chapters, journal articles, and original material. Professor Publishing (Prof Pub) was our breakthrough product. For twenty years, we printed these custom collections of articles and book chapters so college professors could package exactly what they wanted their students to read.

Although we benefitted from rapidly advancing copier technology, Professor Publishing also required lots of labor during brief but intense periods of time. Fortunately, college communities overflow with students seeking part-time employment, except during midterms or finals. This worked for us, because our busiest time was the first week of class.

The first time I worked a store during Prof Pub rush, I stood paralyzed in awe as lines formed around the block.

I was in Berkeley, California, and I remember we used the class schedule to predict which packets would be needed when students poured into the shop after their first class session.

Often, a coworker would hoist a case of Prof Pub readers onto his or her shoulder and cruise the sidewalk, giving anyone paying by check an opportunity to buy their reader and get out of the line. Of course, many of the students were in line to buy two or three or four readers for different classes. As a "packet puller," I spent sixteen hours a day moving like a hummingbird through the tall shelving units jammed into the store's production area and storeroom, collecting finished readers and delivering them to customers at the front counter. For two or three weeks, two or three times a year, Professor Publishing created an avalanche of work and cash—it was a rite of passage that showed us what we could achieve through extremely hard work and how well we would be rewarded for that achievement.

By the way, I experienced this in person because Prof Pub Rush was an "all hands on deck" event. Executives and staff from the partnership offices and Service Corporation were dispatched to stores that needed help—and that was all of them.

We believed that copying materials for educational purposes was consistent with the Fair Use clause of the federal copyright law. In 1991, the Basic Books lawsuit disabused us of that notion and put us out of the Professor Publishing business, but by that time, the stores were outfitted with desktop publishing stations, color copiers, one-hour photo labs, poster printers, and very high-volume black and white copiers, and a third big idea cemented our brand position in commercial and suburban markets as well as university districts: OPEN 24 HOURS.

Through the 1990s we experimented with a number of products and services, including the rental of Apple's primitive digital cameras and our own network of videoconference rooms. Toward the end of that decade, there was no question that the company's retail copying business would be challenged by ever-cheaper laser printers and ever-improving color inkjet printers. The company chose to throw a lot of resources at high-volume commercial printing jobs.

I liked to think that Kinko's overall business model was to provide office technologies to people for whom ownership of those technologies was impractical. Or, as Dan Frederickson put it, "We were a soup kitchen for the technologically homeless." This was true for the senior citizen who just needed to copy his tax return once a year and the company that produced several hundred manuals or handbooks annually. It was even true for a large company like Boeing that had a giant warehouse-sized copy center of its own, but sent overflow work to our Tukwila, Washington, branch. But by 1996, technology was advancing so fast and the company was so big, it was very hard to keep up. By the time we installed new computers in 800 or 900 stores, many customers considered them obsolete. It was clear that the new millennium would present extreme challenges to the business, but we had thousands of smart people working on the problem.

Dean Zatkowsky

Outside the business world, democracy happens when the people demand it. Ironically, the opposite is true within the traditional hierarchy of a business: democracy happens when strong leaders require it. Businesses do not embrace democracy unless the owners behave as benevolent dictators and build structures to engage the population.

Paul Orfalea provided leadership to our company for thirty years, creating an environment of liberty and self-discovery for thousands of smart misfits; Kinko's in the 1970s, 1980s, and 1990s served as graduate school, social club, and extended family for a lot of us who questioned graduate school, craved high-energy friends, and needed a wider selection of cute cousins, weird uncles, and mischievous-but-dependable brothers and sisters. There was definitely something special about the people and the way we worked together.

As I mentioned, there were about a hundred stores when I joined KSC in early 1986. I don't know how many limited partnerships were already in place, but the four big partnerships were established early.

People tended to think of Kinko's Graphics Corporation (KGC) as Paul's company, Kinko's of Georgia (later renamed Southeast Kinko's) as Jim Warren's company, K-Graphics as Tim Stancliffe's company, and Kinko's Northwest (KNW) as Brad Krause's company. This is not exactly correct. Natalie Orfalea, Barbara Warren, Linda Stancliffe, and Stuie Krause were co-owners, co-builders, and integral members of the Kinko's team. The Kinko's partnership ethos grew out of the ultimate partnership model: marriage. (To this day, friends and I discuss whether the Kinko's Philosophy was a Constitution or a wedding vow. It hardly matters which metaphor we use, since each is a bold declaration of shared values).

These four companies maintained a majority ownership in the total company until the "rollup" with Clayton Dubilier & Rice in the late 1990s, but there were other pretty big partnerships, including Kinko's of Ohio (David Vogias), Kinko's of Minnesota (John Thysell), and T. J. Kinko's (Todd Johnson). Small- and medium-sized partnerships were common, and new ones appeared frequently right up until about 1995, as store managers and regional managers opted to open their own territories and build some equity.

We've all spent the last decade reading about jerks who mismanaged their companies, destroyed their coworkers' futures and their shareholders' fortunes, but still managed to leave with heads held high and pockets bulging. (And when I say, "jerk," you know I mean something worse, right?) You also know the type; they cannot distinguish toughness from cruelty, or strategy from whim, and their whole careers consist of asking not what they can build or achieve, but what they can take for themselves.

There are plenty of rude words for the people I'm talking about, but I don't want the crassness of my expressions to derail the story. Briefly, we are talking about self-obsessed supervisors who seem to lack any hint of a conscience. These people exhibit sociopathic tendencies in the workplace, so let's call them Bossiopaths. I'll bet you can think of five from your own work history before you finish this sentence.

Kinko's was a very successful company where Bossiopaths did not rule. Don't get me wrong: they were there, but they did not rule. It was a place where nice guys could work hard and get rich, where high school dropouts could run multi-million-dollar business units, and where smart people dismissive of wealth could do good work, make a decent living, and feel appreciated. It strove to be a genuine meritocracy, where people of varied beliefs and upbringings worked toward commonly understood goals, and those goals were flexible enough to align with each coworker's individual motivation: personal wealth, community service, democratization of technology, or simply the ability to pursue excellence without having to compromise one's ethics. At every meeting with his coworkers, Kinko's Graphics Corporation President Mark Madden captured the overall ethos in a simple, four-word credo: "Have fun. Make money."

In many ways, the company epitomized the upside-down pyramid concept. Customers and frontline coworkers led the organization, Regional Managers and Partners worked to provide resources to the coworkers, and various partnership and corporate offices worked to support the Partners and Regional Managers. Not always and not perfectly, but this was the basic structure. Still, every organization needs a focal point for leadership and management, and as I mentioned before, Paul Orfalea and Dan Frederickson were exemplars of those roles.

Rather than write biographies of Paul and Dan, let me summarize using stereotypes: Paul was a hippie who attended college to avoid military service. Dan was a Marine who served in Vietnam. Paul spent his early career as a hard

E Pluribus Kinko's

partying, brash, loud, entrepreneur. Dan was a sales executive at Xerox. After Paul married Xerox sales executive Natalie Fleet, she suggested that Paul's company could use a presence like Dan's to balance Paul's erratic enthusiasms. (Yes, once again we see the synthesizing intelligence of a woman uniting uncommon elements for a stronger whole. The story of Kinko's success is a strong illustration of the benefits derived from gender-equality in the workplace.)

Throughout his career, Paul always depended on calmer partners to mitigate the disruptive effects of his hyperactivity. In the earliest days of the company, a woman named Dottie Ault filled the role. Prior to Dan's arrival, Kinko's of Washington Partner, Ken Hightower, provided organizational stability. But Dan and Paul were together for a decade of incredible growth, taking the company from a hundred stores to over 1,000 and increasing annual sales from under $100 million to nearly $2 billion.

License to Drive

Dan and Paul were a remarkably effective team because their differences symbolized the range of talents and attitudes of Kinko's diverse coworkers, yet they shared a common management philosophy. As Dan explained,

People like work better when it fits their lives and when employers recognize them as human beings. That Kinko's realized this is phenomenally important. For example, Kinko's understood the importance of family. I worked at Xerox for twelve years. Spouses hated Xerox, because they were treated like outsiders and they only knew the company as something that took away a member of the family. At Kinko's, I knew lots of spouses and family members who weren't coworkers in the company, but they participated in our fun. That's one reason it was a more comfortable place to work.

When I joined the company, Kinko's was already an adolescent of sixteen. Like most American teenagers, Kinko's was eager for its driver's license, and somewhat unprepared for the exciting freedom that license would unleash. The first President of KSC, Ken Hightower, was like our learner's permit; under his leadership we practiced our skills, learned our limits, and got comfortable on the road. He built the Service Corporation into a functional unit. Even though KSC had been created as a provider of services to the partnerships, it was clear from the beginning that, through the Service Corporation, Kinko's was coalescing into something more than the sum of its parts.

When Dan Frederickson took over in April of 1986, he was our license to drive. And drive we did. Young as he was, Dan brought a new maturity and a sense of corporate professionalism to KSC. Which isn't saying much—we

E Pluribus Kinko's

were still pretty wild—but it was enough to get us moving forward as a unit.

I witnessed my favorite example of Dan's leadership skills at a Partner Meeting a few months after his arrival. Dan was addressing the group when, as often happened, a debate broke out among the attendees. Dan stepped away from the podium and let the debate grow for a few minutes. Before long, many people were speaking at once and voices were rising. Dan, still a few feet from the microphone, began speaking quietly and slowly about the topic at hand. Soon, the partners were shushing each other, and then leaning in to hear what Dan was saying.

He regained control of the meeting, addressed the attendees' issues point-by-point, and made one message very clear: "We (KSC) can and will do whatever you want us to do, but you have to tell us clearly what you want us to do." It was a masterful performance by a good leader who, in the same breath, pledged his service and demonstrated his complete control. Dan possessed a quiet confidence that perfectly complemented Paul's loud passion.

I recently mentioned this event to Dan, and he reminded me that he was a musician (Yes, the U.S. Marine and Xerox Executive was a Music major in college and regularly fronted a rock & soul band). He had performed on stage for many years—he knew how to work an audience. At Kinko's University, we studied Warren Bennis' four competencies of leadership. The first is "Manage Attention." Dan had that part wired.

He had to walk a tightrope to do it, but Dan showed us how to become more professional without sacrificing our cultural commitment to open communication.

Paul and Dan also shared a success trait codified by Jim Collins in his excellent book, *Good to Great* (Harper Business, 2001). Both men were ambitious, but their ambition was for the company, not self-aggrandizement. And they both seemed to realize that the company was made of people. I believe this is true of all companies, but especially true of service businesses. Customers may have walked away with physical pieces of paper, but that was not what we sold, really. Paul knew from the beginning that our success depended on the fire in our coworkers' eyes, and he promoted whatever freedoms kept that fire burning.

Dan saw this too, but he took a different tack:

Nothing's more empowering than having the freedom to do what you need to do to get the job done. Coming out of the military, where everybody genuflects to the General, I was surprised that nobody listened to me. Nobody. But then I saw that we could design a framework for success in lieu of command. People could do it or not do it, but good systems, like our national Accounts Receivable program, were adopted on their merits. Remember that each Kinko's was a factory, retail shop, and management office under one roof. Good production and back-office systems freed coworkers to focus on excellent customer service. I felt good because KSC offered something of value to the managers and partners. It was a way to grow the company without sacrificing its character.

The loose-tight framework erred on the side of liberty. Mandates were rare, appearing on a need-to-control basis. Cash controls, for example, were detailed and inviolable. In Kinko's Northwest, cash controls were a "bet your job" area, and managers understood this.

E Pluribus Kinko's

Dan figured out a way to get things done without having to put every idea to a vote. Partners voted on any decision that would be billed to all stores, and the impulse against new expenses would kill many initiatives before they could be tried. Dan got around this by crafting pay-as-you-go services. KSC offered design services, legal services, benefits administration, Workers' Compensation insurance, general ledger, training, and other services. Purchasing, for example, operated like a co-op, and had buying power far beyond the individual store or partnership. Dan got a few partnerships to try these services, report favorably, and soon, the other partnerships would sign up.

Dan needed these pay-as-you-go services to navigate—and sometimes circumvent—the company's complex ownership structure. From 1970 until about 1996, Kinko's was a web of limited partnerships, and every store equaled one vote. In 1996, the partners "rolled-up" into a single company with the hope of going public—remember what IPOs were like in the 1990s? The experts brought in to help with the transition eventually bought out the founding partners and sold Kinko's to FedEx. The post-rollup period is beyond the scope of this book, because I was not there to witness it, and I am unwilling to speculate on what "would have happened" under other circumstances. No one can say what "would have happened."

But to round out the history within the scope of this book, I must note that by 1999, Dan had left the company in disgust and Paul had been banished from his own corporate headquarters. In April of 2000, Paul retired from

Kinko's. It was the first month in the company's history that year-over-year sales declined. This is obviously coincidental, but you have to admit the symbolism is impressive.

As described in the Prologue, I also left the company in 1999, but in 1986, in Santa Barbara, California, I was in the right place at the right time, and got to join these guys for one hell of a ride.

Foundations of Democracy

In 1986, Kinko's Service Corporation was about a year old, and was just one result of a series of decisions from 1983–1985 that would accelerate the company's growth and define the Kinko's culture.

The most important of these was not KSC itself, but was Dr. John Davis's drafting—after a multitude of meetings with coworkers—of the Kinko's Philosophy. The collaborative *process* by which the Philosophy evolved, our focus on coworker development, and the creation of participatory structures all distinguished Kinko's as a company with a bias toward democracy.

Many capitalists shudder at the idea of democracy in business. Owners and executives too often view themselves as plutocrats, holding sway over their business dominion; democracy and communism are equally abhorrent to this elite. Confident in their own omniscience, many focus management efforts on greater efficiency and consistency.

E Pluribus Kinko's

In some businesses, this may be perfectly appropriate, but one size does not fit all.

During the 1980s, one often heard that government should be run more like a business. But you know, government is not a business. In fact, part of the U.S. government's brilliant design is that, unlike parliamentary systems built to get things done, the U.S. system is designed to prevent government from taking too great a role in citizen's lives. I think of the Constitution as the "Congress shall not" document. In our beautiful, messy democratic system, only the most important things should get through the process. The system does not always work the way it should, thanks to our elevation of politics over governance, but it's still a beautiful design for people who love liberty—though, of course, loving *one's own liberty* is not the same as loving *liberty*.

So while Ronald Reagan and his associates preached that government should operate more like business (i.e., based on Theory X, and more ruthlessly efficient, if less democratic), Paul Orfalea thought entrepreneurs should build business models based more on governance (balancing widespread liberty and the common good). But make no mistake about Paul's motives; he sought a fortune—he called it "financial heaven"—and felt that a more democratic structure was the correct path to greater profits in the type of business he was building. For one thing, democracies are inherently more innovative than dictatorships, and Paul's ADHD made him a natural proponent of the "do it, try it" mantra, later codified by Tom Peters' and Bob Waterman's *In Search of Excellence* (Harper and Row, 1982).

It's not that Paul was a social or business philosopher; his trust in the wisdom of the crowd sprang from recognition of his own incompetence. As he often tells audiences, he was blessed with three distinctions: he cannot read well, he can't sit still, and he has no mechanical aptitude. So Paul learned how to appreciate—and exploit, in the best sense of the word—the abilities of others. Imagine an executive who earnestly wants to hear what every worker has to say and is openly grateful for their contributions, and you'll get a glimpse of how Paul's vision of leadership differs from that of most executives. Of course, a lot of early coworkers took this for granted, because they had never worked anywhere else. But I was almost twenty-seven years old when I joined Kinko's and I'd been working continuously since I was fourteen. I knew this place was weird and, very possibly, wonderful.

Kamelot?

My wife insists that I disclose this fact: I complained about Kinko's every day of the nearly fourteen years I worked there. But I hasten to point out that some of us view complaining as evidence of an involved citizenry. In fact, the Dean Zatkowsky Hierarchy of Organizational Contribution ranks "complaining" high above "whining" and just below "useful idea contributions." At the bottom of the hierarchy lies indifference, *the* killer of companies. Compared to indifference, complaining is a pretty good contribution.

I can idealize the past as well as anyone, but I truly believe that people who called themselves Kinko's coworkers between 1970 and 1999 were part of something special, something edifying, something worthy of recognition.

Kinko's existed at an interesting multi-lane intersection of business history. As America made the transition from a manufacturing economy to a service economy, Kinko's stores were little factories providing physical products as services. Later, between the "old economy" and the "new economy,"

E Pluribus Kinko's

Kinko's rented *access* to technology, a service not that different from what you do on the web today.

Kinko's turned me from a quasi-socialist to a lover of business, because the Kinko's culture proved that business could incorporate democratic ideals and still make a lot of money. And it was a fun place to work, pure and simple.

Ideas were the power behind Kinko's success, because Kinko's itself was more a concept than a store, more a business model than a retail business. Our range of products and services changed continuously, and no two orders were exactly alike, which is pretty ironic in a copying business.

Thinkers were welcomed and encouraged. Innovation was a reflex. Our company was a bubbling cauldron of ideas, mixed by a pot-stirrer of epic ability. The struggle of competing organizational ideas was energizing: "store's rights" versus centralized authority, meritocracy versus nepotism, innovation side-by-side with cash-cow worship, customer service expense in conflict with profit percentages, experimentation versus "measurebation," over-confidence versus insecurity (later expertly exploited by the "professionals").

I've loosely categorized Kinko's key success factors under the headings of Philosophy, Partnership Ethos, and Pot-Stirring. I did so to provide some sort of "carrying handles" for the ideas that combined to create the Kinko's Culture. "Culture" is a widely misused idea, but as longtime Kinko's President Dan Frederickson told me, "Culture simply means, 'What's it like to work there?'"

A decade after many of us left the company, I've talked to hundreds of former coworkers who say that Kinko's was the best job they ever had. That's what it was like to work there. I am sometimes accused of being too touchy-feely for a businessperson, so let me remind you that, for the fourteen years I worked at Kinko's, sales grew 30% annually, and we were continuously profitable. It's possible that we were doing something right, even if we were a little idealistic.

Some of the stories sent to me by coworkers from all over the country make up the sections of this book titled "The Coworker's Voice." Many come from people I did not know personally during my tenure at Kinko's, but we have crossed paths on Facebook or LinkedIn or through friends-of-friends when the subject of Kinko's came up. There are tens of thousands of Kinko's stories out there—not all as fawning as mine—but I'm thrilled to share these coworkers' perspectives as illustrations of the democratic pillars on which we built the company:

1. **The Philosophy** was analogous to a Constitution. It laid out our values and top-level rules of conduct. Most importantly, *it affirmed individual rights and common responsibilities*. We put it on display in every store and office, and we printed it on cards for coworkers to carry in their wallets.
2. **The Partnership Ethos** extended throughout the company, far beyond actual equity ownership. Through systems designed to encourage *mentorship, profit sharing, and participation*, coworkers experienced a sense of citizenship.
3. **Pot Stirring** is a pillar of democracy because free speech is as much a duty as a right. We needed candor and we wanted to keep coworkers engaged, so we challenged everything and everybody. *As a*

private company with an exhilarating power struggle between corporate offices and the field, we also relied on a sense of playfulness to keep fences mended and idea-champions healthy for the continuous battle against complacency.

As in America itself, where the highest ideals of mankind are constantly tested by the baser natures of men, Kinko's democratic structure challenged the sensibilities of people intimidated by liberty, responsibility, and equal opportunity. Yet, once there was this bright and shining place; a place where surfers became multi-millionaires, single moms became wealthy business managers, intellectuals were tolerated and encouraged, women and men shared power, and a curly-haired rebel created a culture where disparate people could make a place for themselves while making him and his partners rich. Many of us did not get rich, but most of us were *enriched* by the experience. This was the Kinko's I knew, where a feeling of ownership was not conferred by a stock certificate, but by the liberty to try new things and speak your mind.

Dean Zatkowsky

The Coworker's Voice

Jim (Warren) hired me in 1980. Jim and Barbara were opening stores in the southeast, and they opened the Emory store just down the street from my house. The store was eye-catching—the style then was to have a local sign painter put a huge "4¢ Copies" with "Passport Photos" in orange script on the plate glass window, giving it the look of a tattoo parlor.

Inside, the counters were so rough that splinters were a problem, and the floor was concrete. But who cared? The service was so friendly—it didn't seem like a commercial transaction—that I once forgot to pay and ran out of the store and jumped in the car! Barbara had to run after me. When Barbara told me they were moving back to California, I was crushed, but not surprised, because who could make a business successful four cents at a time? But, no, it seemed they were not closing the store, but would hire a manager and open more stores in time. I don't know why I said, "How about me?" but the work looked like such fun, and I needed a real job. Barbara told me to give them a resume and they'd look it over.

I had no business experience, apart from working in my Dad's store as a teenager, and had never managed anything but PTA programs and community theatre, but the biggest problem I had was my age, forty-three* with two kids. However, I did live just up the block and I did know the community and I did know academia, since I had a master's degree in history and a husband at Georgia Tech. I guess it was enough to get me an interview with Jim, who had been sort of a lurking presence in the back of the store always on the phone and the 9200 at the same time. We went next door to the sub shop and hit it off. Jim never mentioned my age—one of the things I loved about him.

E Pluribus Kinko's

Jim and Barbara left after training me for a month, to go to California, where Jim was to head up Paul's stores. I could not wait for them to go. I wanted to be on my own. I survived that summer and called up one of my housewife friends, Faye Matthews, to take the job as Assistant Manager. Faye had even less experience and no credentials, but I knew her! She ultimately became the most profitable manager (in the country) and a partner in Emory Kinko's. I took my cue from Jim. If he could take a chance on an unorthodox hire, so could I.

Carolyn Gehl, Regional Manager, Southeast Kinko's

*Author's note: Jim and Barbara would have been in their early twenties at the time.

Reviewing Kinko's newsletters from the early 1980s, I saw an interesting trend. The managers, partners, and home office coworkers contributing to the newsletter often seemed to be yearning for each other's company. They presented their ideas to each other and asked for each other's assistance. What's the best way to extend the life of an imaging belt? Who has a good performance appraisal form? How much are you paying for vellum? Overtly or subtly, the fiercely independent citizens of Kinko's wanted to come together; they were looking for help from their peers. Even when Paul started requesting company-wide policies (accounting standards, for example), the emphasis was on unity, economies of scale, and shared burdens. The partners and coworkers loved their liberty, so calls for "consistency" were rare, but everyone was looking for good ideas.

Dean Zatkowsky

In 1983, Kinko's coworkers ratified a set of principles that guaranteed their liberty, codified their shared aspirations, and became the heart of our unique company culture. They called it the Kinko's Philosophy, and it was the first document handed to me when I started work on March 27, 1986.

SECTION 2: BOY AND BUSINESS TAKE A VOW
The Philosophy

The Kinko's Philosophy

Our primary objective is to take care of the customer. We are proud of our ability to serve him or her in a timely and professional manner, and to provide high quality at a reasonable price. We develop long-term relationships that promote mutual growth and prosperity. We value creativity, productivity, and loyalty, and we encourage independent thinking and teamwork.

Our coworkers are the foundation of our success. We consider ourselves part of the Kinko's family. We trust and care for each other, and treat everyone with respect. We openly communicate our accomplishments and mistakes so we can learn from each other. We strive to live balanced lives in work, love and play. We are confident of our future and point with pride to the way we run our business and treat each other.

I remember reading the Kinko's Philosophy on my first day with the company and thinking, "if this is true, this is great." But I wrote screenplays before I came to Kinko's, and one of the key lessons of screenwriting is that people are what they do, not what they say. So that "if" was the proverbial "big IF."

At my second Company Picnic, in June 1987, the company meeting concluded, as most of our meetings did, with a communal recitation of the Kinko's Philosophy. Never comfortable with such cult-like "chanting," I rolled my eyes for the third or fourth time, until I noticed tears streaming down the face of Andra Gordon, a new coworker in the Marketing Department. Andra and I shared an office and worked closely on everything; I wrote copy and she was the graphic artist. As KSC coworkers, we had been working extremely long hours to prepare for the picnic and to pamper our guests from the field, so I understood that any one of us might be in a fragile emotional state. But then I looked around the room and saw a lot of misty eyes.

And it hit me: maybe not everyone in the room believed in the Philosophy, but everyone WANTED to believe in the Philosophy. Everyone in the room had read it the first time and thought, as I did, "If this is true, this is great." For me, the only question after that picnic experience was, "What can I do to make this true?" I never rolled my eyes during the recitation again. Instead, I watched my friends in the audience and marveled at my good fortune. Sometimes, I got a little choked up, too.

The version above appears in Paul Orfalea's book, *Copy This*, as the original Philosophy. I'm not so sure about that. I think the references to teamwork and family were added after I joined Kinko's, because I remember debating the ideas, but maybe we were discussing their removal. The Philosophy was a living document, constantly debated and occasionally changed during my tenure, so it's hard to pin down a single version to represent "THE" Philosophy. Even so, the gist of all versions is here.

"It's Like The Constitution"

Lots of companies craft vision statements because a consultant or book tells them to do so, and these vision statements become legitimate sources of humor and derision. I read somewhere that Dilbert creator Scott Adams pretended to be a consultant and helped a company's leadership develop a vision statement of complete gibberish. (A lot of marketing executives believe they are poets because they care about how each word *sounds*. They don't seem to realize that poets also care about what words *mean*). Many executives just don't get "the vision thing."

A company philosophy is not quite the same as a vision statement, but ours shared some elements. A vision statement lays out where a company is going, while a philosophy expresses how coworkers should behave en route. But at Kinko's, we did not have a tangible vision, because our future was too intricately bound to emerging technologies. To some extent, our Philosophy became our vision, because we believed that behaving honorably in pursuit of prosperity would keep us on the right path, and trite as it may sound, the journey was the destination. Whenever bankers or consultants asked Paul for the company's strategic plan, he handed them The Philosophy.

A vision statement describes a company's aspirations. Unfortunately, many companies' aspirations are too venal to proclaim publicly, so they create poetic, yet meaningless, declarations—"enhancing the human spirit" tripe—that are hung on the wall and promptly ignored—or ridiculed—by coworkers. Rather than unifying coworkers in pursuit of personally satisfying goals, these disingenuous heaps of doggerel simply create another layer of distrust between the organization and its workers.

But some consultants are better than others. A consultant suggested that Kinko's adopt a vision statement, but this fellow understood and cared about the company and its people. Harvard Professor Dr. John Davis studies family-owned businesses and holds a deep appreciation for what people can achieve when they put their hearts and minds to it. Dr. Davis worked with Paul's partners to produce the first draft of the Kinko's Philosophy.

Paul and John describe the creation of the Philosophy in Paul's autobiography, *Copy This*, so I won't go into the history here. Suffice it to say that by 1983, growth was getting out of hand, and the Partners began to wonder how they could preserve the best of their culture while growing so fast.

The Kinko's Philosophy answered that question. Unlike most mission or vision statements, the Kinko's Philosophy became a living document in the organization and directly contributed to Kinko's rapid expansion during the late 1980s and early 1990s.

Having worked with Paul Orfalea for over twenty-three years now, I see that the Kinko's Philosophy existed long before it was written down. John Davis helped codify the ideals already baked into the character of the Kinko's founders. As young men in the 1960s, Paul Orfalea, Brad Krause, Jim Warren, and Tim Stancliffe were used to living outside the lines—and taking heat for it. So they ran their companies with a powerful tolerance for individuals. According to Dan Frederickson, Davis himself argued passionately for preservation of coworker liberty throughout his long association with the company.

I have a lot of affection for a lot of people I met at Kinko's over the years, but Mike Fasth stands alone—friend, mentor, business partner, big brother, and the only coworker whose nose I promised to bloody—neither of us can remember why, but we know it happened on a beach in Maui. Alcohol may have been involved.

When he was President of Kinko's Northwest, Mike and I traveled together often, and, therefore, spent a lot of time chatting in planes, cars, and hotel bars. Mike explained to me that the Philosophy was analogous to the Constitution. "When you have a tough decision, you turn to the Philosophy for guidance, and the decision becomes clear. In all cases, you err on the side of customers and coworkers." Like the Constitution, the Philosophy required frequent reference, discussion, and interpretation, but the document always clarified our focus and affirmed individual rights.

In the early 1980s, our far-flung coworkers and partners sought unity, so they created the Philosophy to say, in effect, "in order to form a more perfect union, we agree to these core beliefs." Indulge me for a few pages while we parse each sentence, so I can show you how the Philosophy asserted itself in our daily work lives.

- **Our Primary Objective is to Take Care of The Customer**

Paul instigated debate and recommended revisions to the Philosophy once or twice a year. Every time the Philosophy was up for revision and reconsideration, Kinko's Northwest (KNW) Partner Brad Krause reminded us to live the Philosophy first, and revise later. I also had a standard response to calls for change: I urged the company to reduce the Philosophy to its first sentence: "Our primary objective is to take care of the customer." I thought that was enough and that smart people could divine the rest on their own. Of course, my real goal was just like Paul's: to get people talking. We attacked the Philosophy periodically to test its defense. Indifference was—and is—the enemy.

"You will never be fired for doing something to help a customer," KNW President Mike Fasth told new coworkers. "We might suggest better ways to handle situations in the future, but when you have to make a choice, choose to help the customer." I thought this was incredibly bold, but trust makes frontline coworkers more effective, and Kinko's—like any democracy—was organized around trust.

We were quite serious about Mike's promise. Author and publisher Dan Poynter sent us an audiotape of a speech he gave about customer service. In it, he detailed how our Santa Cruz location screwed up a large order of booklets he needed for a meeting in Los Angeles. As Poynter explained in his speech, our Santa Cruz coworkers stayed up all night correcting the mistake, and then *drove* the new materials to Poynter's meeting in Los Angeles. Poynter described how the original mistake had enraged him and how our brilliant recovery had delighted him. We promoted this story because we wanted coworkers to think in terms of customers, not orders. We obviously lost a lot of money on that particular order, but we made a lot more money by rebuilding and enhancing our relationship with the customer, who was now retelling the story to audiences of other prospective customers.

Walnut Creek, California, Manager Gina Ruskauff posted a comical sign in her office that defined the word "Triority" as "the three things that must be done first." But at Kinko's, the Philosophy made our primary objective clear. Kinko's stores were very busy places and Kinko's coworkers were the ultimate multi-taskers, but there was no question why everybody was working so hard and so fast: the customers needed them. I mention Gina because one day she broke down in tears and walked out of a meeting with her Regional Manager and me when we criticized the cleanliness of her store. "I'm serving a thousand customers a day and Dean's counting staples in the carpet," Gina said. It was not a difference of opinion; she knew the store needed cleaning, but she needed every minute of every coworker's

E Pluribus Kinko's

day to provide exceptional customer service for those thousand customers. Her priorities were clear and appropriate. Properly cowed, the Regional and I spent the rest of that day and night cleaning the store. We served the people who served the customers.

We made sure that stories of exceptional customer service appeared in the newsletter and every other company communication on a regular basis (and the company newsletter was surprisingly well received in the field—more on that later). We created all kinds of measures and incentives to reward exceptional customer service, because as important as we considered those first words of the Philosophy; only the demonstration of our commitment brought them to life. As Dan Frederickson told me, "The Philosophy hung on the walls of our stores and was printed on cards in our coworkers' wallets. Our job was to walk-the-walk."

Later, Todd Ordal from K-Graphics invented the Service Quality Measurement program, which was quickly adopted by Kinko's Northwest and Southeast Kinko's. The idea was to quantify customer service. We already had metrics like copy average and labor percentage to measure productivity in the stores, but customer service was trickier. Through the Service Quality Measurement program, we called thousands of customers and interviewed them, generating quantitative data (ratings on a 1-5 scale) on qualitative experiences. For example, we asked customers to rate the quality of the product, the speed of the service, the friendliness of the staff, and the overall value. Then we collected comments—thousands of comments. The important thing was that we read them and talked about them and acted on them: We turned the data into information, because our primary objective was to take care of the customer.

The Coworker's Voice

I remember a day in the 1980s when Paul visited Minnesota. I was fairly new. We worked the counter together and a customer had an issue with some copy quality, Paul told me to let the customer have the copies at no charge. I looked at him like, "Hey, we are giving away the store," but the customer was happy and left with a smile. Afterwards, Paul said showing the customer how much we cared is the best commercial we could do! He bet me she would be back and a customer for life.

Bill Miller, Assistant Manager, Minneapolis

- **We are proud of our ability to serve him or her in a timely and professional manner, and to provide high quality at a reasonable price.**

This may seem like a pretty wimpy statement. We don't claim to be the fastest, best, highest quality, cheapest price, etc. To me, though, the genius in this declaration is its connection to "him or her" (i.e., the customer). Timeliness, professionalism, quality, and value are not ours to define: each individual customer carries his or her own view of these qualities. Our job is to meet or exceed their expectations, not to set our own.

So, as a positioning statement, it's not quite the bold stake in the ground; and yet it is. We declare in this sentence that we are comfortable with ambiguity, and that we trust each coworker to bring meaning to these concepts. Coworkers understood that doing one's best is something to be proud of. And managers had talking points for improving productivity: what is timely? What is professional? In a profit-sharing environment, peer pressure influenced the answers more than policy ever could.

Pride is a powerful unifying force, and remember: only hubris or unwarranted, excessive pride is a deadly sin. As Dizzy Dean (the baseball legend, not me) said, "It ain't braggin' if you can do it." We hired our share of cynics in the stores, but by and large, coworkers really did take pride in their daily accomplishments, and the Philosophy reminded us that it ain't hubris if you've earned it.

Dean Zatkowsky

The Coworker's Voice

I worked extra shifts during winter rush at the Eugene downtown store, running machines while the store was closed. I had been employed five or six months at the campus location, had proven some measure of key-op skill, and was the swing shift leader. That was the lowest level of management to be sure, but I felt like I was a full-blown store manager.

This was reinforced when I was given the keys to the downtown store so that I could run copies at night. I worked my eight-hour shift at my store and then worked another six-ish hours downtown, until they opened for the day. I wasn't given specific directions. I was allowed to take as many orders off the table as I thought I could do—and then figured out how to do them. I think I worked five nights in a row and each night I took more copies than the night before. I wanted to challenge my skills and impress the team at MY store.

I made crazy overtime pay, made a ka-jillion copies (how nice to have a clear measure of productivity), but best of all I felt trusted. I walked TALL after that—the partner (Dave Gibson), the manager, and the assistant manager all trusted me to save the bacon during the very busiest time of the year. For a twenty-year-old who had only ever made sandwiches as a job, that was a big deal.

Carl Moyer, Manager, Tukwila, Washington

- **We develop long-term relationships that promote mutual growth and prosperity.**

This is a pretty good introduction to economics, if you ask me. I love that this line introduces the profit motive in amenable terms. We assume prosperity as an objective and present it as an outcome of long-term relationships and mutual growth. Win-win situations are matter-of-factly presented as the norm. There's nothing venal here, but nothing obtuse either: prosperity is our goal, and it is our goal for everyone, including coworkers, vendors, and customers. This sentence serves idealists and greed-heads equally well—and allows both groups to feel good about their efforts.

And of course, "prosperity" is self-defined. Some coworkers sought mansions and exotic sports cars. I sought a comfortable home and a nice collection of guitars and motorcycles. Some just wanted enough money to cover tuition and books. The Philosophy did not define the ends; it only asked us to help each other achieve our personal goals.

Long-term relationships include the coworkers' relationship to customers and the company's relationship to coworkers. So this sentence lays the foundation for fostering customer loyalty (for annuity revenues) and coworker development (for better customer service and, ipso facto, customer loyalty).

The Coworker's Voice

I was just a kid when I became a Kinkoid ... about twenty-one-ish. I say a kid because I was very immature. I was terrified of all the machines and had no self-confidence. I must have fooled

Dean Zatkowsky

Robin, my interviewer/manager. She hired me on the spot and I started the next day.

Over a few months, through her encouragement and training, I became a very good key-op and found myself in that position most often. I learned how to use a computer from scratch at Kinko's. The color copiers were NOT self-serve and we were encouraged to play with them, so we could learn how to make them sing.

We were also encouraged to be out on the floor with customers that had questions and to be helpful, creative, and friendly. We would get little old ladies in and they would drop off their old, precious black and white photos to be color copied in sepia tones. We would get artists to come in at two in the morning and chat us up for hours while we worked and drank coffee.

Robin had these co-worker meetings every couple of months, and she really did a great job of training, teaching, and encouraging me. I was always so pumped to give our store—because it belonged to all of us—my whole heart after one of those meetings.

Carmen Ridge Lewis, Shift Supervisor,
St. Louis, Missouri

E Pluribus Kinko's

- **We value creativity, productivity and loyalty, and we encourage independent thinking and teamwork.**

Ambiguity is a fact of life *and* business. This sentence beautifully captures the paradoxes of a workplace that depends on creativity and innovation, but understands the importance of productivity (to create mutual prosperity).

Managing ambiguity requires maturity. This sentence asks coworkers to recognize that they can be as creative as they want, but they must also perform. Considering how young the average coworker was, this balancing act was tough for many to master. One night in Seattle, a manager tearfully told me she thought she might get fired. She felt it was terribly unfair, because she had come up with lots of new products and operational innovations in her branch. I was familiar with the situation and knew she had been neglecting certain requests from her Regional Manager, including the implementation of ideas from other managers. Moreover, some of her innovations were not working out; the store's copy average (average price) was dropping. I told her, "We love your creativity, but *sometimes* you just have to do what your boss asks you to do." Some people view compromise as weakness or defeat, but compromise can also be an act of genius, a synthesis of ideas that mitigates individual arrogance.

She hung in there, opened a new store for us, and left a couple years later on her own terms. Choosing to open the new store was a step down in pay for her, but put her energy and creativity in the right place. She was lucky, in my opinion, to work with a Regional Manager who appreciated her talents and strove to find the right place in the organization for her.

When I think of balancing independent thinking and teamwork, I recall Stephen Ambrose's book, *Citizen Soldiers* (Simon & Schuster, 1998). This grunts' history of World War II shows how individual soldiers used their ingenuity and improvisational skills to advance the "team's" objectives. Kinko's coworkers were not engaged in a war—we weren't even that concerned with industry competitors. But we were competing with our customers' expectations, which presented new challenges every day in every store. Our "citizen soldiers" were empowered to use their judgment, but were also encouraged to share their discoveries and learn from each other.

The Coworker's Voice

I always got better results from people by letting them do things their own way rather than prescribing, and I sometimes think all our efforts (mine included) to write manuals and enforce complicated systems turned out to be a waste of time. They didn't help those who needed them and weren't needed by those who could help themselves.

Carolyn Gehl, Regional Manager, Southeast Kinko's

Think about the paradox: an organization of individuals. Such an organization cannot abide Bossiopaths—or more accurately—Bossiopaths cannot abide such organizations, where supervisors must respect their coworkers. But even those who faithfully embrace the ideals of teamwork and independent thinking struggle with the subtleties.

At one meeting, a Regional Manager told her store managers that coworkers should resolve customer complaints by giving them "whatever they want, within reason." Another Regional Manager told his coworkers to give unhappy customers "whatever they want, period." In effect, both had said the same thing, but the qualifier, "within reason," left coworkers plagued with questions about their boundaries, because they had to wonder what their supervisor would consider "within reason." She unwittingly placed an obstacle between her coworkers and exceptional customer service. The other Regional's statement did not result in coworkers giving the store away. Rather, it empowered them to use their own reasoning skills. He demonstrated that he trusted them to use good judgment. (This is not a knock on the first Regional, who taught me how to deliver powerful and productive performance appraisals. It's just an illustration of how tricky it can be to promote independent thinking in the workplace. Many people learn early in their careers to prioritize pleasing their boss over pleasing their customers.)

I find it interesting that "loyalty" is sandwiched between the two sets of paradoxical ideas. Clearly, this does not refer to blind loyalty, or we could not value independent thinking. I don't think it refers to the company, either, since we were big believers in free agency. No, I think this was about loyalty to our values, such as our primary objective and the encouragement of independent thinking and teamwork. And perhaps more important: loyalty to one's coworkers. Interviews reveal that soldiers find meaning not in the slogans and propaganda of their cause, but in the protection of their buddies. The rest of the Philosophy is almost entirely dedicated to this idea.

- **Our coworkers are the foundation of our success.**

The meta-message of this point makes clear that recognition is a means to an end—and the end is success of the business. Paul is refreshingly honest when he says that happy fingers ring happy registers.

Now, this is exactly the sort of sentence that gets eyes rolling. That's why we did so much to recognize coworker contributions publicly ("Caught In The Act" rewards, idea contests, etc.) and to spread profit sharing as far into the organization as partners could bear. This is also why we worked so hard to ensure coworkers' voices were heard. We wanted coworkers on committees and the board of directors. We traveled ceaselessly and spent our time in stores, chatting with everyone we could find.

Toward the end, I traveled with Paul Orfalea and the late Andrall Pearson (former Pepsico CEO, McKenzie & Co., partner, and CDR affiliate) to field questions from coworkers at meetings in Seattle and Portland. The coworkers were very vocal about their ambivalence toward the impending rollup, our opening of stores in China, dress codes, etc. Paul enjoyed engaging the coworkers in debate and making his points (e.g., you don't help China by ignoring it). Pearson's attitude struck me as one of bemusement. He cheerfully endured the coworker meetings and I think he genuinely appreciated what the company had achieved on its own. But I think he was unaccustomed to the breadth of open communication in our company.

Consider the literal interpretation of *foundation*—the base upon which everything else stands. The broader the base, the more stable the edifice. Coworkers are in fact the foundation of every business, but when you say it out

E Pluribus Kinko's

loud, you commit to engagement with those coworkers. As you'll see in the *Participation* section of this book, Kinko's provided ample opportunity for engagement.

Most people know Winston Churchill's most famous quotation about democracy, that it is the worst form of government except for all the others that have been tried. His second most famous quotation about democracy goes like this: "The best argument against democracy is a five-minute conversation with the average voter." I did not find this to be the case at Kinko's. I spent three-days-a-week in stores, hanging out with coworkers. We disagreed on many individual points, but the aggregate education was invaluable, and I think most Kinko's executives felt the same way. Of course, unlike democratic nations, we were able to interview and *choose* our citizens.

I recently told Dan and Paul how ironic it was that I had conducted marketing training workshops all over the country, when I was the one who was actually getting an education from managers, regional managers, and frontline coworkers. "No," said Paul, "that's just what happens when you hire naturally curious people. We wanted people who were interested in learning from everyone and every thing."

We polled the stores to the point of annoyance and beyond, because no one knew more about customers than our coworkers—sometimes they knew more than the customers themselves. And coworkers were the people who knew how to run the machines and invent solutions. Coworkers were the foundation of our success because they were the foundation of knowledge and ability. Once again, I draw your attention to the company's origins: Paul Orfalea's dyslexia and ADHD made him dependent on and appreciative of others. This line of the Philosophy codifies not only an "upside-down pyramid" of management priority, but also an understanding that *we depend upon one another* to succeed. We are all coworkers, and we are all in this together. The company is its people.

The Coworker's Voice

In 1985, I had been working for Kinko's for less than two years when my six-year-old son Jonas suffered a blood-related crisis that put him in the hospital for a week, with multiple blood transfusions and a diagnosis that surgery was necessary. Kinko's had no co-worker health insurance at the time.

Although most of that episode is a blur, I distinctly remember my Regional Manager at the time, Peggy VanWaard, there by my side at the hospital. The bills from the hospital stay and treatment and upcoming surgery were imposing, to say the least, and I honestly had no idea where the money would come from. I remember going to the picnic that summer and getting off the bus at the hotel. There was Paul greeting the managers and shaking everyone's hand, as he always did at the picnic.

I had met him perhaps two or three times. The first thing he said to me as he shook my hand was "I heard about your son and I want to let you know, I'm going to take care of it." My immediate reaction was something to the effect of "Paul, you can't do that, it's thousands of dollars!" His comment to me was, "I don't want you to be under that kind of stress." Obviously, Peggy had let Jim Warren know about the situation and it had gone from Jim to Paul. To make a long story short, I never saw a hospital bill and was never questioned by anyone about how the bills would be paid. It was just taken care of. For the many years I worked with Paul

E Pluribus Kinko's

after that, whenever I saw him he always asked me first thing, "How's Jonas?"

Years later, after the company rollup, Paul came to the University of Illinois to give a talk about entrepreneurship for the MBA program. Many Kinko's coworkers from the surrounding area came to hear the talk, as well as my son and my now daughter-in-law Katie, who were students at the U of I. When Paul came out he immediately went into the audience and started shaking hands and talking with people in the front rows. When he came to Katie and introduced himself, she said, "Here's someone you might know; this is Jonas." I will never forget the look on Paul's face as he stepped back, eyes wide and a big smile, and said, "Jonas?! Where's your Dad?" After the talk, Jonas and Katie had a chance to talk briefly with Paul and thank him personally for what he had done for us.

I have been blessed with a truly wonderful and healthy son, and now a beautiful baby granddaughter, and not a day goes by that I don't count my blessings.

If you want people to care and be passionate, then, as a leader, you have to care and be passionate. It's not something you can fake. The founding partners cared and were passionate about the growth and profitably of business, but more important they truly cared about the people they worked with, customers and coworkers, within that context. These are people who didn't need a document to tell them to care about and treat people like family. This is who they are. It's what they brought to the table. That was the magic that Paul, Brad, Jim, and Tim were able to cast. The fact they were able to create an environment that perpetuated and encouraged these qualities, and quite literally changed the lives of thousands of people is a legacy of which to be truly proud. In a world where so

Dean Zatkowsky

many businesses only care about profit, and are careless, or couldn't care less about the lives of the coworkers and customers, Kinko's was different, and better. I feel incredibly lucky to have been a part of that.

Jim Downey, Regional Manager, Kinko's Graphics Corporation

E Pluribus Kinko's

- **We consider ourselves part of the Kinko's family.**

A brilliant young man named John Huffman joined us in the Marketing Department in the late 1980s. It was he who told me that when you call a business a family, you degrade the otherwise noble concepts of business and family. I liked this, because, early in my career, I rolled my eyes every time someone referred to the company as a family. In the beginning, all I could see was hierarchy and privilege. To me, family meant nepotism.

One day in 1987, I met with Paul to discuss a newsletter article and to complain about my boss—I was always complaining in those days. Paul seemed to agree with me while somehow not agreeing to do anything about it, saying only that I should remember that the company is a family.

Frustrated by Paul's evasiveness, I repeated John Huffman's position, that when you equate business and family, you degrade them both. Paul responded, "You know why I say we're a family? Because you can pick your friends, but you're stuck with your family."

I didn't like that answer, because it meant that I was stuck with all the people I didn't like, all the people who didn't meet my standards for competency and intelligence and kindness. But after a minute or so, standing there silent and sullen, it dawned on me.

"They're stuck with me, too."

Paul didn't respond, unless you count the smile. It was a liberating moment, to say the least. Stuck with each other, we had to learn to appreciate each other's talents and abide one another's foibles.

Also, the family of my family is my family, right? Nonprofit organizations were always approaching Kinko's for donations, but Paul insisted that charity starts at *home*, so we had scholarships for coworkers' children, 401(k) plans, extensive healthcare benefits, free Friday lunches at the corporate office, etc.

Dan Frederickson says that if you build a cocoon of safety for coworkers, "You can let them go at it and they'll grind out whatever has to be done." The *family* concept was that cocoon of safety. Robert Frost wrote, "Home is where, when you have to go there, they have to take you in." By creating a sense of family, we created a sense of home in the workplace. We could try new things, fail, and still come home.

The Coworker's Voice

Back in the day, we used to get paid between the 1st and the 5th of the month, then again between the 15th and the 20th. That could make it pretty tight by the 20th. One manager I had, Jeff Goldsmith in Birmingham, MI, bought a full-sized fridge for the break room. He would stock it about three days before payday with REAL food. Enough to feed the store at least one meal a day. That "family" mentality isn't found in many places.

Carrie Gaddess Mudge, Assistant Manager,
Birmingham, Michigan

- We trust and care for each other, and treat everyone with respect.

Kurt Vonnegut, Jr., said that the world would benefit from a little less love and a lot more respect. When you believe in liberty, independent thinking, and open communication, you cannot stress respect enough. About a year or two after its creation, we supplemented the Philosophy with our Commitments to Communication, which enumerated behavioral guidelines that would help us live by the Philosophy:

Commitments to Communication

I will recognize your value to Kinko's.
I will share my goals with you and together we will develop an action plan.
I will respect and utilize the chain of command to resolve problems.
I will solicit immediate feedback to assure we understand each other.
I will talk with you, not at you.
I will listen with an open mind.
I will try to see the situation from all points of view.
I will tell you when I don't know the answer and together we will seek the answer.
I will give you honest and sincere feedback.
I will not usurp your authority.
I will not confront you when I am angry.
I will not gossip.
I will not publicly embarrass you.

I will admit when I am wrong.
...and in every case, I am worthy of the same from you.

Most people reading this list make their own mental list of their coworkers' daily violations of these commitments. I confess that we all had problems living up to these responsibilities, but tell the truth, wouldn't you like these standards to be the goal in your workplace?

Once, when I was visiting a store in Portland, Oregon, I noticed that they had "modified" the commitments poster. The two changes I remember were, "I will not gossip, but do you want to know who does?" and "I will not usurp your Slurpee." The manager was embarrassed, but I was laughing my head off. I didn't care about the poster; I cared about modeling these behaviors for the coworkers.

Many coworkers knew the language of the Philosophy and the Commitments to Communication, as I learned every time I breached them. But that is precisely what helped many of us grow as leaders, becoming less temperamental and more rational in our debates. Respect makes conflict **USEFUL**.

- We openly communicate our accomplishments and mistakes so we can learn from one another.

If I could get politicians to learn one thing from Kinko's, it would be this. Part of the magic here is the opportunity for fast failure, an *In Search of Excellence* trait required in a "do it, try it" environment. There's no point in experimentation, if you cling desperately to your mistakes. And there's no chance for personal growth if you overstate the impact of mistakes. I wouldn't say that anything that doesn't kill you makes you stronger, but I would say that anything that doesn't kill you doesn't kill you, so get back to work.

I transferred to Kinko's Northwest division in 1988, the year Tom Peters published *Thriving on Chaos* (Random House, 1988). As it happens, Kinko's of Georgia partner Jim Warren had a ticket for a Tom Peters event but could not go, so Kinko's Northwest Operations VP Mike Fasth went in his place. Mike got very fired up, and soon everyone in Kinko's Northwest was reading *Thriving on Chaos*. We were already fans of *In Search of Excellence* and there was no question we were operating in a very chaotic environment, so we chose to embrace that chaos in a very bold way.

We wanted to offer Nordstrom-quality service even though we often sold a five-cent product. Store managers convinced us that our strict payroll percentage limits prevented them from adequately staffing the stores, so we tried a new model: forget about labor percentages, hire as many people as you need to provide exceptional customer service! We were eager to see what would happen.

A few months later, Mike and I were standing outside the Menlo Park, California store, watching the results.

A bevy of coworkers gathered behind the counter. As customers approached, the coworkers retreated. The coworker who didn't back up fast enough took care of the customers, but usually it was the manager, Angie Walsh, who zoomed in and did all the work. We saw similar behavior in many stores; we had staffed up, but hadn't devoted adequate resources to training. Nor had we modified our procedures. Our "Glue System" for operations was designed to keep a lean staff attached to specific responsibilities, reducing the physical steps required to move a project through the store. Extra people were gumming up the works.

A few months after that, Mike and I were in Seattle when we got the call from Brad Krause: *The experiment has cost a million dollars and isn't working; stop it today.* So we reinstituted labor percentages and returned to lean, efficient staffing. But Mike points out that "our million dollar mistake was a brilliant mistake. It showed our need for a training function outside the stores, it showed that fundamental metrics cannot be ignored, and it showed our managers that we listened and were willing to try their suggestions. All of these made us more successful in the nineties." This was not mere spin: we admitted the mistakes, discussed alternatives, and grew through the process.

This part of the Philosophy also reminds us to practice forgiveness. I once ran a magazine ad that featured a naked baby on her father's lap. It was part of my "Who do you really work for?" campaign, which promoted Kinko's as a way to finish your work faster so you could spend time with your family. Well, the proximity of a naked baby and a man's bare legs caused an incredible uproar. We got dozens

E Pluribus Kinko's

of complaints, including threats of physical violence for promoting child-rape. I thought these complainers were the sick ones, seeing horror and depravity in an obviously benign scene. My enemies in the organization (Let's be clear; this book is about key success factors and messy democracy, not an idyllic utopia.) seized on the opportunity to condemn my "irresponsibility," demand my head, and lobby for centralization of all advertising.

I took a lot of heat and turned to Sales VP Greg Soulages, an IBM veteran experienced in the ways of more conventionally political workplaces. I asked what he would do in the event of such an obviously insolvable conflict. "Declare victory and move on," said Greg. I thought about it.

Eventually, I went to Paul for advice. He was aware of the situation. He shrugged, said, "You tried something. It didn't work." In other words, I didn't have to declare victory, but I had to move on.

That was the end of the controversy, as far as I was concerned, and a triumph of the Philosophy over office politics.

- We strive to live balanced lives in work, love and play.

Our training and educational programs reinforced the importance of a balanced life. Copies of USC Professor Warren Bennis' article, "Four Competencies of Leadership," circulated liberally, and many of us carried it to our post-Kinko's workplaces as well. I still have a copy (legally purchased!) in my file cabinet. Dr. John Davis led workshops on the four competencies at Kinko's University. I included them myself, as an added bonus, when I conducted marketing workshops. I still believe they provide a great touchstone for people who wish to be good leaders, regardless of their title, scope of authority, or personal style.

The four competencies are: 1) Managing Attention, 2) Managing Meaning, 3) Managing Trust, and 4) Managing Yourself. A balanced life helps with number four. Too many "leaders" work themselves (and their staff) to a frazzle. They become haggard and anxious. But most of us do not aspire to be haggard and anxious, so why would we want to follow such a leader? As Kinko's of Washington partner Ken Hightower told coworkers at the 1987 Partner Meeting in New Orleans, "It's okay to take a lunch break. It's okay to go pick up your dry cleaning." A good business shouldn't kill you.

It's hard to remember a Paul Orfalea speech from the 1980s or early 1990s that did not include a reference to this tripod of work, love, and play. These speeches were about managing ourselves. Paul would rest three fingers on the podium and illustrate the strength when all three legs of a tripod were of equal length. He didn't tell us how to find balance in our lives, but he constantly reminded us that it was important, and that the company KNEW it was important.

Of course, a lot of young, ambitious people voluntarily turned the balanced tripod of love, work, and play into a pogo stick, as in, "Hey, I love my work and I'd like to play with that cute coworker over there...." But when push came to shove and a coworker needed time with an ailing relative or a "mental health day," we turned to the Philosophy and remembered to take care of ourselves—and each other.

In a thousand Kinko's stores, managers sought ways to provide respite and balance for their hardworking coworkers. One of our Marin County stores featured a deck over a stream. Manager Tony Kasprzyk provided fishing poles so coworkers on break could relax and do some fishing. At our corporate offices in Ventura, we had basketball courts, a running track, a softball diamond, and the Little K-Kids daycare center.

The Coworker's Voice

Little K-Kids was a big part of the culture and I am ever grateful to Paul and Natalie for this commitment to families. There were five of us in Marketing that had babies around the same time—so we would take turns going down to K-kids, playing and holding each other's kids.

Mary Sequoia Hamilton, Kinko's Service Corporation

- **We are confident of our future and point with pride to the way we run our business and treat each other.**

Again, the word "pride" shows up. The last sentence suggests we can be confident of our future *because* of the way we run our business and treat each other. The Philosophy concludes by suggesting that living by this Philosophy imbues our efforts with moral authority. I remain a true believer and this line of the Philosophy captures the reason. I'll illustrate with a movie reference.

In an early Sam Peckinpah western called *Ride The High Country*, two aging, former lawmen take a job transporting gold from a mountain mining camp to the bank in the town below. One of them wants to steal the gold; he feels cheated after years of sacrificing his life and health for an ungrateful society. He asks his old partner, Steve Judd, whether they deserve better for all their years of service. Judd replies, "All I want is to enter my house justified."

I've always felt the Kinko's Philosophy provided coworkers a code for pursuing the gold *and* entering our houses justified. I think it was the ultimate expression of enlightened capitalism—and pretty damned profitable, too.

Later, we supplemented this sentence with a reference to "the environment," after Greenpeace raised a ruckus and showed us ways to run the business with greater sensitivity to the environment. Now I know there are some people who believe that sins of omission are as bad as sins of commission, but I do not subscribe to that philosophy. Naiveté is no crime. We were a bunch of relatively inexperienced people, focused on making money. When Greenpeace picketed our stores, we didn't say, "Go away!" We said, "Show us how to

E Pluribus Kinko's

do this better." We were not ashamed of our naiveté. We were willing to listen and learn when someone thought we were doing wrong.

Explaining why he never had trouble finding new co-workers, Moscow, Idaho, Manager Tim Eaton once told me, "It's a clean place to work, literally and figuratively."

A Living Document

The Philosophy was always under review and Paul, the pot-stirrer, made sure it was a topic of conversation in our committees, conclaves, newsletters, etc. It would be bad enough if the document were hung on the wall and ridiculed, but far worse if it were hung on the wall and forgotten or ignored. Paul made sure the Philosophy was top of mind.

But anyone who knows Paul might also question how his legendary temper and impatience squared with the Philosophy, particularly its veneration of coworkers. The answer is simple: Kinko's Philosophy and hierarchy were designed not to rule over coworkers, but to protect them. KSC and the partnership offices served as a buffer. According to Mark Madden, who held just about every possible job at Kinko's, including President of Kinko's Graphics Corporation (Paul's partnership):

{Kinko's of Long Beach partner} Charlie Wright, {K-Graphics President} Todd Ordal, and I were at the Turfway racetrack in

E Pluribus Kinko's

northern Kentucky with Paul and some of his horseracing friends and we'd had a lot to drink. One of Paul's friends challenged him, wondering how someone with his volatile personality could run something as complex as Kinko's.

"I treat the managers like gods," said Paul. "I lavish them with praise and attention."

Doubtful, the friend asked about me, Charlie, and Todd, "What about these guys?"

"Oh, they're meat," said Paul with a wicked grin. When his friend looked over, the three of us were nodding.

One thinks of Ernest Hemingway's description of the bull corrals in Pamplona, Spain, where steers were introduced, so the bulls would have something to gore.

In the field, Paul would spend half an hour praising a manager for having "the best store I've ever seen," then leave twenty messages for the partner, pointing out everything that was wrong with the store—and the partner. I don't think this was hypocritical, because I believe Paul attributed whatever was good in the store to the manager and coworkers and whatever was wrong in the store to the partnership and management bureaucracy. And according to our Philosophy, he was correct, more or less.

Dean Zatkowsky

The Coworker's Voice

I recall Paul constantly asking all of us to challenge the Kinko's Philosophy and the Commitments to Communication (CTC) via the Newsletter and other methods ... bringing it up out of nowhere in speeches, at the Picnic, etc. The Philosophy and CTC were core to our company's daily behavior and overall direction. I remember Copy Consultants and others in the stores reciting these important words. Ten years after my departure from Kinko's, I still have the business-card-sized document in my wallet, containing the Philosophy on one side and the CTC on the other. Isn't the last sentence on the CTC perfect? " ... and in every case, I am worthy of the same from you."

... as I was responsible for managing conflict and performance counseling for KGC for three years, I recall how co-workers relied on the Philosophy and CTC in their daily lives. On many occasions, I would receive calls or complaints from co-workers citing how their manager or some other employee violated the CTC or Philosophy and they were upset about it. Co-workers expected life at Kinko's to be consistent and compliant with these words. After all, they read about it in the Co-worker Handbook upon hiring. When managers were clearly not living the Philosophy and CTC, they were firmly counseled or terminated. I know the front line co-workers appreciated this very much.

Nick Shauer, Human Resources, Kinko's
Western Division

Unambiguously Paradoxical

The Kinko's Philosophy was open to interpretation, yet strangely unambiguous. It encouraged creativity and leveled the playing field by declaring our values and, in effect, daring anyone to violate them. It expressed the rights of the citizenry.

Another essential feature of the Philosophy was that it encompassed everyone who touched the company, including our vendors. From giants like Xerox and Kodak to small firms like Stetson Security, we tried to treat everyone like a Kinko's citizen.

The Philosophy is preeminent among Kinko's key success factors, because it allowed us to understand one another's values and trust each other's judgment. Everyone knew the rules, and that allowed 25,000 coworkers to bring their best game to work every day, because they could be themselves and still work toward our shared goals.

When I left the company, I destroyed or left behind all of my Picnic memory books, but Mike Fasth lent me some of his to spark my memory for this book. Page six of the 1995 *Picnic Yearbook* offers two versions of the Philosophy: the version that opened this chapter and a revision proposed by the board of directors. The primary recommendation: remove "independent thinking" from our list of values. I don't remember whether the change was voted in, but I don't think it mattered. The fact that the board of directors even suggested this change signaled the beginning of the end for the Kinko's culture.

The Coworker's Voice

I have never seen an organization that took these kinds of documents/statements as seriously as Kinko's. The fact that there was always discussion about the adequacy of this word or that speaks volumes. Many companies arrive at a mission statement or a philosophy, but it has no real meaning to the team. I would say that a significant percentage of co-workers understood the spirit of the Philosophy and the Commitments to Communication and tried to live them. My sense is that co-workers who survived for more than a couple of years really bought into those documents ... because they make so much sense.

Eric Schwarz, Finance VP, Kinko's
Graphics Corporation

SECTION 3: BOY AND BUSINESS GROW TOGETHER
The Partnership Ethos

Limited Partnerships of Unlimited Potential

During my first month with the company, I held down the marketing department fort in Santa Barbara while everyone else attended a sales meeting in Chicago. One day, I got a call from a fellow with a thick drawl. He wanted to buy a Kinko's store for his daughter. I explained that we were not a franchise, but a series of limited partnerships. "I don't care what it costs," he replied. I repeatedly explained that we were not a franchise, but then I realized I didn't fully understand how the partnership structure worked. Did you have to meet Paul in a bar to become a partner? Well, sometimes.

Paul Orfalea designed Kinko's as a series of "Sub-S" partnerships. This distributed equity—and prevented the double-taxation that C-corps experience. Paul held an ownership stake in each store. Paul's partnership company was called Kinko's Graphics Corporation, and those stores were 100% his. In other partnerships, he might own 51%, or 50%, or as little as 10% when partners spun-off new companies for their Managers and Regional Managers. Most partners worked their way into a partnership opportunity; only a rare handful bought their way in. As the organization grew, some executives failed their way into partnerships, as befits a family business.

The partnership structure encouraged fast growth. In the beginning, it cost very little to open a store because we leased all the equipment, got partner/hippie/carpenters to build the furniture, and rented small commercial spaces in university districts. Later, it became very expensive to open a branch (5000+ square feet, custom designed cabinetry, premium locations, etc.), but we had our own bank—new partners could borrow money from the company to open a store. Once we really hit our stride, Dan says all a new partner needed to open a store was a location and a checking account. The Service Corporation provided capital, design, cabinetry, machines, etc.

Paul wanted localized ownership for better management, and he wanted owners to have their own "skin in the game." He knew that people risking only his money would be less motivated than people risking their own. He also wanted partners who knew how to save money. And yes, this is why I never became a partner. As I often tell friends, during my peak earning years I spent most of my money on cameras, guitars, and motorcycles, but I squandered a lot too....

So, no, you couldn't just buy a Kinko's partnership. Except when you could. It was up to the people with whom you wanted to be partners.

Over time, the partners stratified based on the number of stores owned: the Senior/Large partners—Paul Orfalea,

Jim Warren, Brad Krause, and Tim Stancliffe—owned fifty or more stores each; small partners owned one, two, or three stores; and medium partners made up the numbers in between. And of course, there was some multi-level marketing at work, as partners subdivided their own territories to provide opportunities for their coworkers. Thus, Brad Krause's Kinko's Northwest owned seventy branches (in partnership with Paul), but Kinko's Northwest itself was also a partner in Kinko's of San Jose, Kinko's of Napa, Golden State Kinko's, and many others.

There were also "micro-partners." I was one. Paul and Dan wanted co-workers at the Service Corporation to have ownership opportunities without leaving to run a store, so partners made small percentages of certain stores available for purchase. I owned two percent of Kinko's of Buffalo, which was a partnership between Toledo store manager Ted Vrahoites and Kinko's of Ohio partner David Vogias. When I left Kinko's Service Corporation, a year after investing, David insisted that I sell the shares back to him, so he could offer them to Kinko's of Ohio staff. Although I made a small profit on the shares, the overall experience was a net loss because of the extra expense I incurred for tax accounting. Keep in mind that, at that time, my annual income as a KSC Advertising Manager was probably less than some managers' monthly profit sharing checks, so that was my last foray into the realm of Kinko's partnership.

The Sub-S partnership structure definitely achieved its goal of fast growth—we added about 900 stores during my tenure—but the system created difficulties, too. For example, many of us at Kinko's Northwest were frustrated that

E Pluribus Kinko's

the Kinko's of San Jose partnership did not expand, even though its community grew dramatically in population and wealth during the 1980s and 1990s. We surrounded the territory with stores to take advantage of Silicon Valley's explosive growth, and I'm sure we cannibalized the partner's business, but someone had to serve those customers. We experienced some similar stress in Oregon, as we opened stores on the periphery of another partner's territory. I'm sure this happened all over the country.

From Paul's perspective, there were also quite a few problem partners—people who refused to invest in their stores, or to respect the company Philosophy, or participate in advancing the larger organization. He remembers his Kinko's years as a 24/7/365 struggle, and to this day, I can ruin a meeting by mentioning certain names to him (a handy distraction when I don't want to discuss something else). He thinks fondly of the partners and coworkers who dissented and debated to advance their own points of view, but he still gets very worked up when recalling anyone whose store was a "pig sty." (Cleanliness and order are real hot-button issues with Paul. He often said that going into a Kinko's with bits of paper on the floor was like going into a hospital with puddles of blood on the floor—it instantly undermines a customer's confidence).

The partnership structure allowed the company to grow fast, but it included no exit plan. In the mid-1990s, the senior partners' conversations turned more and more toward what they wanted to do in their forties and fifties. According to Dan, K-Graphics partner Tim Stancliffe, in particular, wanted out, but there was absolutely no mechanism for it.

No clear methodology existed for valuing the business, and as I mentioned before, the partners were bound together by financial exposure.

Leverage played a huge role in the early years: partners tapped home equity or borrowed from their parents and friends to get a store going. As a campus-based business, cash flow was tenuous. We had two huge peaks during fall and spring with Professor Publishing. In December, we usually had to lay off coworkers. Fortunately, we had the bank of Xerox. Xerox's billing department was so disorganized that Kinko's ended up owing far more—in the tens of millions of dollars—than anyone would have lent us up front.

Paul often guaranteed loans for his partners and this was a tremendous source of stress. All those loan guarantees influenced Paul's decision to partner with Clayton, Dubilier and Rice in the 1990s. Soon after the separate partnerships were combined into a single company, I was traveling with Paul and mentioned that I'd never seen him so relaxed. He explained that, until the rollup, he had worried every day that he could lose *everything*.

A Wide Range of Talent and Ability

Paul selected partners he felt he could trust, regardless of their ability. Over time, the variety of partners illustrated the wide range of talent, ability, and trustworthiness that one might expect in any large group of people. One fellow was nicknamed "The Magician" for his ability to turn money into shit. On the other hand, Paul called Kinko's Northwest Regional Manager and Golden State Kinko's partner, Tom Parrish, "Moneybags," because of his stores' profitability.

In the early stages of the partnership rollup, I became Marketing Director for the Western Division and got to visit some stores I'd never seen when they belonged to small partnerships. At first, several of us displayed our arrogance, expressing dismay at the way other companies had been managed. For example, when former Kinko's Northwest co-workers visited stores in McAllen and Brownsville, Texas, we scoffed at the fact that these giant stores in tiny markets had EVERYTHING: Videoconferencing, perfect binding,

E Pluribus Kinko's

gold foil stamping, etc. Our first impression was that partner Phil Schlageter just couldn't say "no." In fact, Phil made decisions based on population density. The towns were small, but the service area for the stores was huge. His two stores did not offer more services than other groups of stores serving similar populations. When I worked at KSC and KHQ, we often viewed small partnerships as recalcitrant fiefdoms, but *local ownership meant local understanding.*

Free agency was another benefit of the partnership structure. Coworkers moving around the country found their skills in demand in almost any community. The variety of separate partnerships and leadership styles also meant we could find a company culture best aligned with our own sensibilities, and partners could recruit experienced coworkers from one another. "Career Corner" was an enormously popular newsletter feature.

Obviously, free agency was as much a point of contention as a benefit to the partners, but it was of great advantage to the coworkers. Sales VP Greg Soulages, Finance VP Ross Waddell, and I all migrated from Kinko's Service Corporation to Kinko's Northwest. Paul and Dan complained that Northwest cherry-picked talent from KSC (referring to Ross and Greg—not me!), but KSC also attracted talent from the field, as executives and for ad hoc projects that benefitted from the massive talent pool.

One downside of free agency, according to Dan, was that we could not allocate talent where it might have done the company more good. Noting we were slow to develop Professor Publishing at the large, wealthy schools in the Northeast, Dan speculates that a single company would have redeployed a successful Regional Manager, like Tom Parrish, from the San Francisco region of Kinko's Northwest. In our partnership structure, the relationships made such moves too complicated and raised loyalty issues.

Kinko's Northwest was sometimes called the "Playboy Partnership," because Brad Krause was a strikingly handsome, physically fit man who surfed, windsurfed, raced cars, collected cars, rode motorcycles, held management meetings in Maui, and mixed a mean Kamikaze. But the greatest strength of Brad's company culture was that he was a good leader who refused to micromanage his coworkers. We set goals together, and then he simply expected us to do what we said we were going to do. Whenever I asked, "What's my budget?" Brad replied, "What do you need to do the job?"

The coworkers at Kinko's Northwest loved working with Brad and the same kinds of relationships were formed throughout the kingdom, as it were. Southeast Kinko's coworkers loved working with Jim Warren. T.J. Kinko's coworkers loved working with Todd Johnson, and so on. We were different bands of the same tribe. Each partnership had its origin myths, hero myths, hardship myths, etc.—stories that defined who we were and who we aspired to be.

The variety of cultures could have been divisive, but the overarching culture made us friendly—albeit fierce—competitors working toward a common goal of profitability. According to Dan Frederickson, "There were a hundred partner cultures, plus the overall culture, plus the KSC culture, but there was maybe a 20-30% overlap, and that was enough to make us a growth machine."

E Pluribus Kinko's

A significant portion of the cultural overlap was the trickle-down partnership ethos. In addition to the patronage aspect described above—where partners took on new partners and mentored them—there were two other essential elements to the partnership ethos that drove success: *Profit-Sharing* and *Participation*. These enabled coworkers without literal shares of ownership to share important benefits of ownership: financial opportunity and a voice in their future.

Profit-Sharing

Virginia Woolf claimed that she first submitted an article for publication because she wanted a cat and selling an article allowed her to buy a cat. After that success, she decided she wanted an automobile ... and a literary career was born.

In 1987, I wanted a Fender Stratocaster.

I was still with Kinko's Service Corporation when I took part in a Kinko's of Ohio meeting in Kent. I conducted my little marketing workshop, and then I attended their business meeting, which included the announcement of store sales records and the disbursement of monthly bonus checks. Since the previous months included the beginning of the school year and sales from Professor Publishing, one of the managers received a bonus check for over $12,000. At the time, that was about half of my annual salary. When he showed me a picture of the Fender Stratocaster he planned to buy, I instantly transformed from laid-back quasi-socialist to ambitious capitalist. I wanted to make big money and

E Pluribus Kinko's

buy guitars too, and Kinko's seemed like a good place to do so. My career took a turn at this point, because I realized that the big money was out "in the field," not at the Service Corporation.

David Vogias owned Kinko's of Ohio, and over drinks, he raised the possibility of my leaving KSC to join his partnership as Marketing Manager. By this point, I was pretty frustrated with my job, but had only considered leaving the company altogether.

I generally use this story to explain my difficulty working for Charley Williams: Because we had to provide the stores a huge variety of ads, they accused us of providing marketing materials by the pound. But every store had different services and different hours, so we tried to create ads for each of them. At least quarterly, I had to write a minimum of a hundred print ads. One time, I turned in a set to Charley and his written comments included gems like "Excuse me while I throw up." We met and he explained that he wanted more creative and dynamic headlines. I said it was more important to express benefit statements in the headlines. He demanded that I produce a hundred new ads—overnight.

I stayed up all night and, indeed, created a hundred more exciting and creative headlines, fueled by pure anger. Reviewing them the next day, Charley looked me in the eye and without a trace of irony asked, "Don't you think that headlines should always include benefit statements?" This sort of thing seemed to happen almost every day, although with the benefit of hindsight and the mellowing effect of age, I now concede that I probably misunderstood and/or exaggerated a lot of our conflicts.

Finding a marketing position within Kinko's, but outside the marketing department, had not occurred to me, because, at the time, none existed. Then, K-Graphics (the partnership centered in Colorado, with stores throughout the Midwest) hired Bill Capsalis as a partnership-level marketing manager. And there I was, going partnership-to-partnership, teaching marketing techniques to managers. Dr. Z's Traveling Marketing & Medicine Show turned into a *market Dr. Z to the partners* show. I wanted a piece of the action.

Businesses invent all kinds of complex incentive systems to influence coworker behavior, but it seems to me that a simple profit-sharing program achieves the greatest feat of all: it aligns everyone's interests around the organization's reason for existence. No incentive program replaces engaged management, and simple plans require just as much vigilance as elaborate ones. But widespread profit sharing gets everyone looking in the same direction.

Profit sharing engages coworkers in the whole life of the business. They learn about fixed and variable costs, customer acquisition and retention costs, overhead, etc. And they learn about the cost—and value—of labor. During one of my visits to Arcata, California, partner Craig Redwine and I were going out to lunch. He told me that a prospective coworker was coming in for an interview, so I suggested we reschedule lunch. He laughed and explained that his coworkers would handle the interview. "Every new coworker affects everyone else's profit-sharing check. We only hire new people when it's absolutely necessary, and they make sure we only hire people who will pull their own weight. They're way more selective than I would be."

Because there were no illusions about our goal (not to be confused with our primary objective—customer service—which helped us achieve our goal), there was less of the management hypocrisy that so often divides workplaces. Paul in particular was not shy about saying that we were in it for the money. "You can give yours away," he would tell coworkers, "but the organization exists to generate profits." That kind of candor goes a long way toward helping young people understand capitalism.

The Coworker's Voice

I started at Houston III in 1987 making minimum wage—I'm pretty sure that was $4.35 an hour. I thought it was just another throwaway job until I saw my manager's monthly bonus check, which had five digits to the left of the decimal point. Five years later, mine did, too. What a great company!

From the start, I was amazed at how many truly brilliant people worked at Kinko's. I did a poll once at Houston III. Of something like twenty-five coworkers, six were national merit scholars. That's about twice the percentage of Harvard's incoming freshman class. In my humble opinion, the fact that it was able to attract and recruit talent far beyond what one would expect for any sort of retail business was the foundation of Kinko's success. Kinko's was able to do so for so long because it explicitly trusted the judgment of its coworkers.

Smart people don't like being treated as if they were idiots. Before I came to Kinko's, I'd worked at least a dozen retail jobs where it was plain my employers didn't think I could pour piss out of a boot unless instructions were written on the heel. When I started at Kinko's, my managers (and later Paul) handed me a stack of expensive equipment and said, "Figure out how to use this stuff to help customers." That kind of trust is really breathtaking in an employer. Today, my clients pay hundreds of dollars an hour for my advice on billion-dollar transactions, but my employer still doesn't afford me the autonomy that Kinko's did when they paid me $4.35 an hour. Go figure.

Barry Jacobs, Manager, New York IV

E Pluribus Kinko's

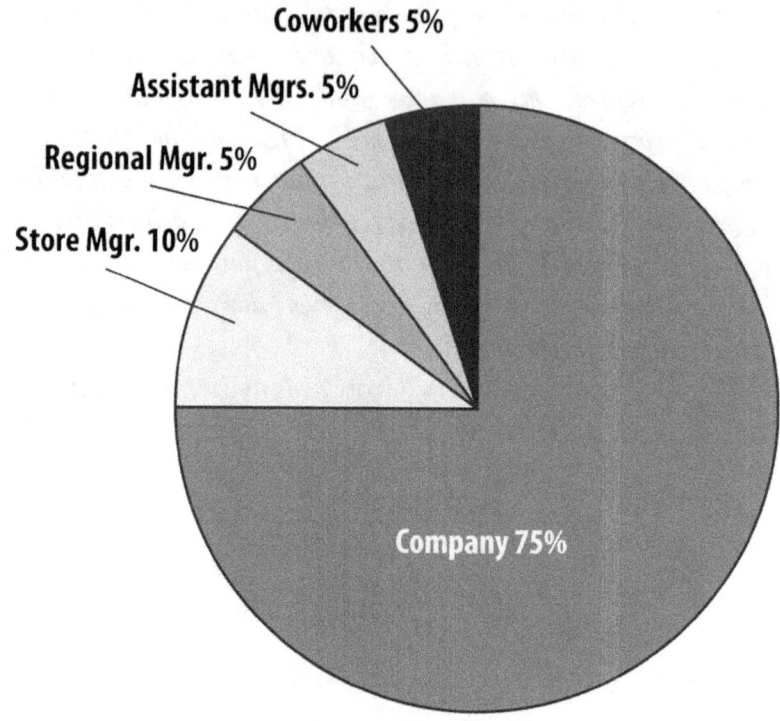

Store Level Profit Distribution

Keep in mind that this is a chart of distributable profits, which the coworkers received as income but the partners generally poured back into the company. The formula differed at various partnerships and changed over time, but on average, approximately 20% of a branch's profits went to the team at the store. This focused a lot of attention on each store's P&L statement, inspired coworkers to seek promotion, and even helped to hold partners more accountable for their contributions to each store's success. (Originally, profit sharing of 25% was just for managers, but over time we saw that broadening the distribution served everyone's interests. By and large, the managers were very frugal people—they were good managers because they understood the value of a dollar. After many years of saving her money and building her store, Angie Walsh of Menlo Park, California, finally treated herself to a BMW with personalized plates that read NOMRVWS.)

Ambassadors of Capitalism

Many people see any economic unfairness in the United States as an indictment of capitalism itself, but I think this is just as misguided and needlessly simplistic as the idea that "government is the problem, not the solution." That we have incompetently managed our government and our economy proves only that we have been careless and irresponsible in our stewardship of two great and noble ideas. Capitalism and representative democracy remain worthy goals. Business owners can do much to support them.

I've heard conservative pundits accuse academia of turning young people against capitalism, but I don't believe it. As an old marketing guy, I'm convinced that brands are formed by experience, not advertising. Many young people are indeed turned against capitalism, but not by their professors. Young people are turned against capitalism by their first experiences in the workplace.

Incompetent supervisors and mendacious business owners do more harm to capitalism than Karl Marx ever did. They create an adversarial relationship with people who could be their partners, and that makes things harder for every other employer. I think capitalism thrives when people entering the workforce are encouraged toward entrepreneurship. And the best encouragement is a taste of ownership.

I'm a staunch supporter of generous profit sharing because I think every business owner benefits from mentoring coworkers and teaching them how business works. Profit sharing is not so much a share-the-wealth program as a share-the-knowledge-and-responsibility program. The wondrous thing about profit sharing, as we learned at Kinko's, is that the owner gets a slightly smaller slice of a MUCH bigger pie when all coworkers' interests are aligned. When the economy struggles, you're going to need partners in your business, not adversaries.

Many years ago, I addressed a class of business school seniors who accused Kinko's of gouging customers because we charged so much to send faxes. The students had considered the cost of the fax machine, the cost of the paper, and the cost of long-distance telephone calls, but that was all. Seniors in business school had not considered the cost of rent, the cost of personnel, the cost of electricity, advertising, taxes, health care, etc. Where will they learn these things?

Profit sharing requires one to open the books so coworkers can see where profit comes from and where profits are lost. So this is not a good choice for venal, dishonest owners; but it is a way for respectable business people to fight against the perversion of capitalism and to produce future generations of honest, generous business owners. The workplace is the best environment for business education, and if we believe that capitalism is worth saving, we must give our coworkers tangible evidence of its benefits.

Dean Zatkowsky

The Coworker's Voice

I view Adam Smith's "invisible hand" as one that beckons with incentives, but some others view it as an iron fist wielding capital like a brutish club. The latter certainly give capitalism a bad name, but embarrassed capitalists also cause harm. These are the leaders and managers ashamed to admit they want to make money. I have never been shy about my interest in money; I am a money enthusiast. But the best way to make a lot of money is to help people—coworkers and customers—get things they need and want. I learned from experience that kissing coworkers' hands made me more money than slapping them. Iron-fist capitalists see profit distributed to coworkers as money left on the table. They believe that if they can take it, it is rightfully theirs. This is shortsighted and counterproductive.

And that's why so many workers deride capitalism itself. Their personal experience suggests the invisible hand is less than benign. As one humorist put it, "Some see the hand everywhere they look; others see only one finger." Profit sharing makes the invisible hand visible and welcoming, and serves capitalism well.

Paul Orfalea, Founder, Kinko's

Controlling Costs Without Cutting Corners

Paul railed against waste on a regular, very public basis, leaving angry voicemail messages about wasted postage and unnecessary four-color printing.

Seattle Manager Scot Winn sat on a broken office chair for years. To meet with Scot meant you either had to get used to the thirty-degree angle at which he was sitting or tilt yourself to look him in the eye. Every time we met, I worried that he was hurting his back and begged him to buy a new chair. He said he didn't mind, and he liked the message it sent to his coworkers.

When Hawaii Regional Manager Ron Kuhn didn't like the construction bids he got for removal of a wall, he waited until his building manager went on vacation. Then he rented equipment and took out the wall himself.

Throughout the company, profit sharing inspired frugality, but sometimes to a fault. Managing the behavioral impact of a profit sharing plan is more challenging than designing the financial incentive in the first place. Among

E Pluribus Kinko's

inexperienced business people, profit sharing leads to the unintended consequence of excessive scrimping.

Frugality fuels profitability, but not when we trip over dollars to pick up pennies. Anyone offering profit sharing to coworkers must ensure they understand the big difference between cutting costs and cutting corners: the former improves profits; the latter eventually destroys them.

Coworkers new to profit sharing often focus on transactions instead of customers, trying to maximize the profit immediately visible to them. But the customer is far more important than the transaction. At Kinko's Northwest, we taught that each transaction should include an incentive to encourage the customer's next transaction. We tried to make sure coworkers understood the lifetime value of a customer.

During a store meeting in Palo Alto, California, manager Tim Smith showed his coworkers a stack of crookedly cut and badly bound booklets that had been "hidden" in a case about to be delivered to the customer.

"I don't know who did this," said Tim, "but I have to ask: Who were you hiding these from? Did you think the customer wasn't going to see the booklets they ordered? Did you think it didn't matter once we got paid? This was cowardly, foolish, and just plain wrong. And it's bad business."

Darn right. With few exceptions, customers become more profitable with every visit. To make profit sharing an incentive for growth, we must constantly reinforce the difference between good profits (annuities from recurring customers) and bad profits (a quick buck without regard for the customer relationship). A bad profit today leaves you without a customer tomorrow.

To provide a simple illustration of the value of repeat customers, divide the total cost of customer acquisition—from your marketing expenses to your customer service personnel—by the number of new customers each year. Show how each repeat visit or referral works off that cost and increases overall profitability. Customers become more profitable over time for many reasons, but the acquisition cost is easily calculated and understood by coworkers. It also helps to keep the marketing department honest.

If profit sharing is presented as an end in itself, corner cutting becomes the company culture and undermines our ability to generate profit. Instead, show that profit sharing is the outcome of efforts to provide excellent customer service. Managed vigilantly, profit sharing aligns the interests of owners, coworkers, and customers. Unmanaged, profit sharing turns them into mercenaries working at cross-purposes.

For the most part, partners did not mind investing in their managers and their stores. In the late 1980s, Dennis Itule, who held a share of most of the Los Angeles area stores, told me that, while some partners were living extravagantly on their cash flow, he still believed in pouring everything back into the business. He understood that profit sharing was an investment in equity growth. The partnership *feeling* extended throughout the company but, ultimately, the actual partners were paying others to grow their equity for them. Kinko's profit sharing may have seemed like generosity, but it was above all a growth strategy.

The Coworker's Voice

At the Las Vegas Maryland Parkway store, we had three key ops with a collective fifty years experience. The classic profit sharing model linked shares to seniority, so these folks, who were doing work they enjoyed doing, were highly compensated compared to similar positions in other shops. Experience turned these Key Ops into expert problem solvers of great value to commercial customers and other bread & butter accounts, the ones that needed quality, speed, and the peace of mind that comes from working with people you know and trust.

Scotty Perkins, Technology Specialist, Kinko's Corporate Office

Some people roll their eyes at the idea of retail employees as "expert problem solvers," but Scotty points out, "Kinko's was absolutely not Burger King. At Burger King, you can have it your way, but still must choose from the fixed menu of ingredients. At Kinko's, every single job was a unique creation and people even brought in their own ingredients. What we were doing was HARD! The unlimited permutations required high quality, experienced coworkers, and you frankly do not get such people at low hourly rates."

Ripples of Prosperity

Early in my tenure at Kinko's Northwest, a group of executives, managers, assistant managers, and regional managers were dining in San Francisco. It was a festive conclusion to a long day of meetings, but I wasn't feeling very jovial. Everybody had worked hard, but my list of post-meeting action items was longer than most, and looking around the room, I realized I was the lowest paid person there. I was handling all the advertising, merchandising, and product rollouts for fifty or sixty stores, but even the assistant managers in the room were making a lot more money. I didn't feel it was unfair, because I believed in the store-centric model, but I was bummed and I let my boss, Mike Fasth, know that I wanted to make more money. We weren't real keen on title and position inflation, but we were big believers in ambition and opportunity.

Kinko's Northwest Regional Manager Steve Williams had always told me that if I wanted to make more money, all I had to do was come to the operations side of the business.

But I liked marketing and viewed it as my calling. Mike and Brad appreciated this and thought about solutions, not just for me, but also for others in the home office.

The partnership ethos in general and profit sharing in particular helped the Kinko's companies practice something later codified by Jim Collins in *Good to Great*. Collins noted that the best leaders put together teams with a "first who, then what" philosophy. That is to say, like Charley Williams in the Marketing Department, they hired for attitude and ability, and then figured out what responsibilities each person could best take on.

Recently, I heard from a former Kinko's manager who now owns a copy and print shop, and I asked how he brought the Kinko's Philosophy to his current venture. Kraig Schexnayder owns DocuCentre in Covington, LA (www.docucentre.net) and told me that profit-sharing was key to achieving his goals:

The Coworker's Voice

The profit-sharing structure was the backbone and the most integral aspect of my success with Kinko's. There was no having to "buy in" to ownership—it was really there. Your hard work and success was directly compensated, as though that branch was your own. At DocuCentre, although just "turning the corner," we have the very same structure—salary and 10% profit for manager, 5% for assistant manager, and shares for full time coworkers.

Profit sharing has allowed me to pursue a vision of opening other DocuCentres in larger markets, since my role as owner is different than it would be as owner-manager. Of course, it initially costs me more to have a manager in place at the infancy of this business, but profit sharing has provided my manager with the responsibility of ownership. It also allows for more candid and effective decision making, since we collaborate and make decisions, which I find more useful than me just "taking ideas."

Kraig Schexnayder, Manager, Baton Rouge, Louisiana

Kraig also told me that he keeps a small refrigerator near the front counter and offers customers complementary soft drinks while they wait for orders to be completed. Former Kinko's Northwest President Mike Fasth always told me that the greatest secret of retail success is this: be nice to people. Sometimes, it really seems like a secret, doesn't it?

Lowering The Bottom Line

One of the biggest problems with Kinko's profit sharing plan was that we didn't charge back for bad debt, so managers had no incentive to cut off or follow-up with slow- or non-payers. I remember a manager of the Berkeley store telling me she couldn't cut off UC Berkeley, despite the fact that their account included $140k over 90 days past due. "They're my best customer," she insisted. "No," I explained. "Your best customer pays you."

This raises another difficulty of profit sharing—calculating profit in a fair and understandable way that advances everyone's goals. What type of losses should carry forward and for how long? Do bad debts get charged back to the store, or does the company eat them? How much corporate overhead is charged to each store? Is it calculated as a percentage of sales or a flat rate? How much detail do you share? Many of these factors were continuously negotiated as stores grew and conditions changed.

E Pluribus Kinko's

In 1986, Finance VP Ross Waddell explained the beauty of Kinko's to me: "A store's fixed costs run about $30,000 a month. After that, you're making upwards of 90% profit." The low breakeven was a result of our built-in frugality, because everyone in the company was watching the P&L. But, as the organization grew, so did the number of people whose compensation was not tied to the store P&L. Just eight years after my conversation with Ross, Carl Moyer opened the monstrously huge Tukwila, Washington, store for Kinko's Northwest.

The Coworker's Voice

I joked then, and still do, that I got the manager job because no one else applied for it. Bellevue had total sales in the neighborhood of $200k per month, but of the thirty-ish stores in Puget Sound, none had ever had sales of the size needed to make money in a branch like Tukwila.

We expected to start the branch with a $200k break-even (more than the largest store did in total sales!), but it ended up being $240k (first full month) and climbing in the first year to $270k. That's when I began to see how many different groups were feeding at the trough. I remember discovering the price of the cabinets. If I recall at all correctly, it was $5-6k per month (for five years) on the P&L just for furniture.

*The push for uniformity was making the financial side more challenging. And **every** part of the branch had something that was like that. I felt at many points that everyone got to make money before the store did. It was a big change from the Eugene branch or even from my first management gig on Capitol Hill (a neighborhood in Seattle)*

Carl Moyer, Manager, Tukwila, Washington

Dean Zatkowsky

After breakeven, we still generated over 90% gross margins, but the stores had to support an ever-growing corporate structure. I was always part of the problem, because I was always "overhead." No matter how much we tried to expand the concept of partnership, there was always conflict between those above and below the line on a store's P&L.

After the rollup, profit sharing was seen less as an incentive program than as a profit leak.

The Coworker's Voice

The beginning of the end of my tenure with Kinko's started once I was given goals that disregarded my input, and I got a tremendous boost in salary, but very low target compensation from goals. For some, that was a good thing—in the end, the pay was almost the same, and with a larger salary there was more comfort. For me, it took away the competitive edge that always fueled me. ... (At my new company,) we share all of our P&L information with the group. It is exciting to hear conversations built around core costs, focusing on goals, etc. These were the very same conversations I used to hear in my more profitable Kinko's branches.

Kraig Schexnayder, Manager, Baton Rouge, Louisiana

Compensation Alone Does Not Create Engagement

Profit sharing inspired meritocracy (like the hiring process in Arcata) and corruption (like the corner-cutting episode in Palo Alto). I cannot emphasize enough that profit sharing's benefits to the company were not an automatic, mechanical result of paying people a percentage of their store's profit.

Our managers, assistant managers, and coworkers typically earned more than their peers at other organizations, but that didn't buy us better coworkers. It only bought us the opportunity to hire better coworkers. The secret to paying people more is to hire and retain people who will earn it. And to really know the people in your organization, you must spend time with them. One of my favorite management quotations, for which I regrettably have lost the source, says, "You can pretend to care, but you can't pretend to be there." Face time matters.

E Pluribus Kinko's

We kept the profit sharing plan simple and devoted resources to person-to-person mentorship. And the really nice thing about mentorship at Kinko's was that it was always a two-way street. When Mike Fasth was President and I was Marketing Director at Kinko's Northwest, we spent 50% of our time in stores. This was not uncommon in the partnership offices, because each partner had started with a single store and knew where the action was. Sometimes we were teachers, but always we were students. And more important, as we worked the self-serve area or attended store meetings or stayed up all night saddle-stapling booklets, we were *citizen coworkers*.

A friend told me that to survive, a democracy must guarantee two things: opportunity and justice. This enhanced my view of Kinko's as a democratic institution, because I saw the Philosophy and the Partnership Ethos as vehicles of justice and opportunity. I think the Philosophy's role is obvious: it defined our parameters of justice. The patronage and profit sharing elements of the partnership ethos clearly promoted opportunity. But the really powerful democratizing factor at Kinko's was coworker *participation*. If we erected a tombstone to the Kinko's brand, I would carve an epitaph that reads: "Where every coworker had a voice."

Participation

Despite my lack of experience when I first joined the company, I quickly recognized that I was better educated than many Kinko's partners, and, just as quickly, I adopted an arrogant attitude: "How did these people get so far without me?" In retrospect, I realize that everyone who joined the company after the first two or three stores probably felt this way. Karen Sophiea replaced Charley Williams as VP of Marketing in 1989 or 1990, and she must have believed that her experience at large companies like Heinz would transform the company's apparent chaos into a more conventionally professional organization. After the rollup, a new VP took over the Marketing Department (at Kinko's Corporate Office; the pretense of a "service" company was long gone at that point), she was not shy about telling me that our previous success (over 900 stores and almost $2B in sales) was dumb luck. Kinko's Northwest in particular, she assured me, was only successful because of geography. She didn't just wonder, "How did they get so far without me?" she asked us point blank, even though she meant it as a rhetorical question.

The new leaders may have marveled at our chaos, but we marveled at the fact that the company's growth stopped cold upon their arrival. Besides, the condition perceived as "chaos" by outsiders was in fact just a combination of messy democracy and market forces.

In *Copy This*, Dr. John Davis told of attending a partner meeting and the fact that he had never before seen "... organic Republicans... They were capitalist hippies, really." Mike Fasth reinforces the point: "I don't know how serious a businessman Brad Krause portrayed himself to be, because he dressed casually and yeah he was a surfer, but he was a businessman. He had the understanding and the vision; he knew the numbers and he valued the people."

The Kinko's partners weren't just Capitalists; they were American Capitalists, and Idealist Hippie American Capitalists, at that. So they set up the structure of Kinko's to ensure their voices would be heard. I realized at my first partner meeting that I wasn't just watching business presentations—I was watching political campaigning. Now, that's true of every business presentation, to a point. But most VPs conducting a PowerPoint presentation are selling a proposal to their board or management team. At Kinko's, our presentations had to buy us votes *in the field*, because there were as many votes as there were stores. The partners were as much representatives of their managers as they were independent owners.

It's true that Paul controlled a majority influence in the company and some people said of the system, "We keep voting until Paul gets his way." But I did not find this to be the case. Yes, Paul fought hard for the things he wanted, but so did other partners. Plus, the culture reflexively rebelled against top-down dictates, usually successfully. Field enthusiasm—or lack thereof—could make or break a new product.

At Kinko's Northwest, we experimented quite a bit with speed of profitability for new products and services. We developed a Service Implementation Process focused around one question: if we could get coworkers excited and educated about a new product in the months before it arrived, could we generate profitable sales on that product in its first month in the stores? We didn't just lecture to them about, for example, the first Apple Color LaserWriter. We involved coworkers in the process by challenging them to devise the best way to implement the product in THEIR store. And we didn't end up with fifty or seventy different approaches—the best two or three won out as the coworkers sold each other on their ideas. When it came to credibility, store coworkers trusted each other far more than they trusted visitors from "corporate." So we simply created the opportunity for coworkers to get educated and excited, taking advantage of a population of people self-selected through the curiosity and enthusiasm in their DNA.

Keep in mind that the partners in general—and Paul in particular—could slam-dunk any decision, if they so pleased. But we saw that kind of behavior as self-defeating, because if you can dictate anything, you demoralize your coworkers and then you have to dictate everything. This saps the organization of innovation and enthusiasm, two critical

E Pluribus Kinko's

components of growth. Worse, it requires a top-heavy organization, and before you know it, you're General Motors—completely out of touch with the world around you.

In our democratic structure, coworkers had the option of voting with their feet. Operations VP Karen Madden reminded me, "Dictatorial partners quickly lost their best people to 'better' partners."

I wouldn't say that the partners were on their best behavior at the meetings I attended. I'd say they were on their only behavior: boisterous with occasional gusts of pugnacity. I liked it. But here's the really weird part, even when I'd been with the company just a few months, the owners kept asking my opinion. Part of the partnership ethos driving the company was a fervent belief that, when it came to ideas and opinions, the more the merrier.

On one level, this was a mark of insecurity, because many of the partners doubted their own ability and sought help for every decision. But over time, we became secure in our belief that broad participation was the *right* management style for our company. Paul Orfalea is as strong-willed and stubborn a man as you are likely to meet, but he recognized, along with his partners, the value of generating a critical mass of ideas. Out of quantity comes quality. This drives efficiency freaks crazy (crazier?), but one should never trade effectiveness for efficiency.

I wouldn't go so far as to say that insecurity itself was a key success factor at Kinko's, because it also led to our capitulation to Clayton, Dubilier and Rice, but Paul's childhood difficulties with ADHD and dyslexia left him with an "anyone can do it better" philosophy. He needed to empower others in his organization, and for the most part it worked really well. Frontline empowerment and broad coworker participation were responses to our insecurity, and these were indeed key success factors.

Kinko's obsession with coworker participation generated a lot of ideas, including some great ones, from Open 24 Hours to custom color calendars to ever-improving production systems. It also produced widespread buy-in for the best ideas by involving a huge cross-section of the company in the development of those ideas. Partner Alan Adler and his team in Oklahoma pioneered the market for courtroom presentations, while Corky Manns and his team in Salt Lake City devised systems for efficient copying of legal discovery documents. Greg Clark in Utah and Glenn Carter in California created personalized direct-mail businesses based on the Kinko's platform.

Bumper stickers proclaim that the best way to predict the future is to help create the future. Kinko's created and nurtured an innovative environment by allowing coworkers to participate in change. Paul's "anyone else can do it better" ethos blessed Kinko's with an impulse to welcome broad input. Over the next few pages, I'll describe just some of the forums used by coworkers at every level of the organization to share ideas and help create the company's future.

E Pluribus Kinko's

KSC Committees and Board of Directors

The departments at Kinko's Service Corporation met with advisory committees composed of managers, regional managers, partners, and staff elected by their peers. These committees were remarkably powerful, because they influenced what initiatives would come up for partner votes, and partner votes controlled the purse strings for projects like national advertising or the Academic Courseware Exchange (a 1986 joint venture with Apple Computer, intended to replace textbooks with course materials on floppy diskettes! The program—twenty years ahead of its time—was led by Keith Lawrenz.).

Store managers serving on committees took their representative role seriously and were enthusiastic about soliciting feedback from their peers. They also provided a direct conduit to their own day-to-day experiences. Scott Wattenbarger managed the Stockton store for many years. When the Operations Committee took on the company-wide problem of paper inventory management, Scott described how he tracked and managed the wide variety of papers jammed into the back room of his store. Scott assigned codes to streamline the long names of the various types of paper. The codes were integrated into order systems, paper sample books, and storage shelves. The system reduced miscommunication at the counter and allowed coworkers to see at a glance which paper supplies were running low. It wasn't brilliant or revolutionary; it was just well organized and efficient. Most stores had some kind of system, but other members of the committee considered this a best practice.

Voila! The Wattenbarger Paper System was rolled out to the stores. Naturally, there was resistance from those who had created their own systems, but over time the Wattenbarger system prevailed if only because Purchasing adopted the paper name codes. Some complained that the Wattenbarger System was a top-down mandate to the stores, and that was partially true, but the idea rose up from the stores, excited the Operations Committee, and they charged KSC with the responsibility for promoting the system back to the stores.

When I mentioned this to Paul, he recalled only the conflict and resistance he had encountered in the field. Since I spent most of my career at Kinko's Northwest, which generally adopted ideas quickly, I'm not really sure how much resistance there was in the field. I traveled quite a bit and rarely saw it myself. I think the greater problem for Paul was that he was the one who had to deal with recalcitrant partners and managers. So even if 90+% of the company quickly embraced a new idea, Paul remembers the few he had to fight. Dan adds some perspective, however, when he says it felt like he had to fight for everything.

As I recall, the Wattenbarger System was the only method or product named after a coworker. Scott took a lot of teasing—some playful and some malicious—over this. Based in part on Scott's experience, we recognized future contributors anecdotally, rather than by naming things after them. Besides, most innovations at Kinko's were simultaneously discovered at dozens or hundreds of stores and were often suggested by customers.

The KSC board of directors included representatives from small, medium, and large partnerships, outside directors like Dr. John Davis, and of course, Chairperson Paul Orfalea. Eventually, the board also included a store manager.

I think the board was especially important to the small and medium partners. They did not have the votes to overrule the large partners, but a strong board representative could influence what made it to the ballot.

In advance of board or committee meetings, representatives polled their peers. People inevitably get sick of surveys, but the opportunity to be heard was always there.

Partner Meetings

I have no idea why I was able to attend so many partner meetings over the years, considering my experience as a partner consisted of owning a two-percent share of Kinko's of Buffalo for less than two years. As a coworker at KSC, I sometimes had to present or support a presenter from the marketing department. After my move to Kinko's Northwest, I think Brad simply recognized these meetings as opportunities for networked learning; like Paul, Brad knew that good ideas were everywhere, and he wanted his team out where the ideas could be found. We also held our own company meetings in conjunction with the partner meetings, so we could get a quick start executing decisions from the larger group.

Inclusiveness made the partner meetings more effective. For the most part, the meetings were open to those of us who were not partners. At coffee breaks and meals, I got to learn how people in smaller companies or other parts of the country ran their businesses and I got to share what was working for us. The meetings built knowledge and empathy.

One of my favorite partner meeting exchanges took place during a heated debate over a decision to require neon price signs in the stores. K-Graphics partner Tim Stancliffe staunchly opposed the signs and kept lobbying against the motion. It wasn't just a question of aesthetics, although many managers believed neon signs belonged in bars, not business service centers. It was primarily an economic issue: the stores would have to buy the signs, which reduced their profits, which affected every coworker in the store a little bit, and the managers a lot. I think for Tim, it was also a

E Pluribus Kinko's

marketing issue, because we preached that Kinko's should not compete on price, but now we asked stores to advertise their base copy price. When it seemed clear that the motion to require the signs had enough votes to win, Tim's frustration grew. "What am I supposed to do—fire a manager who doesn't want to hang the sign?"

Kinko's of Chicago partner Theresa Thompson had had enough and raised her voice over the chattering crowd, "It's not that hard, Tim. If you want, I'll send my dog over to show you how to do it." Call it rude, call it unprofessional, but don't call it ineffective. The filibuster ended, the partners voted, and the signs were shipped. I have no idea whether the signs were hung in Tim's stores, but if other managers and regional managers liked them and felt the signs increased sales, Tim's regional managers would have gotten the news quickly, either through the newsletter's list of monthly store records or at one of our periodic conclaves.

Regional Meetings/Conclaves

These were some of the most exciting and productive meetings, even if they did not always appear so. Many of us complained about the volumes of binders produced at these meetings, because so few of the proposals in those binders got implemented in the stores. But I have to admit that the regional meetings proved that out of quantity comes quality: the best ideas got implemented because their advantages were self-evident. The sheer number of good ideas that didn't get implemented serves as evidence of the vibrant, creative environment. When it came to engaged, enthusiastic contributions, we suffered an embarrassment of riches at the Regional Meetings.

As the company grew, Regional Managers developed huge spans of control. Moreover, many of them were small partners. By the late 1980s, regional and partner meetings were often combined and called Conclaves. Typically, we would convene in a city with numerous stores and devote at least one day to store tours. Often, it seemed we chose conclave locations to encourage remodels and upgrades to older stores. The smell of fresh paint was not uncommon on these tours.

Usually, we opened with an educational and/or inspirational keynote address and then broke into small groups to work on specific issues raised by customers or coworkers—phone etiquette, front counter communications, packaging, signage, etc. Some former coworkers must have shelves and shelves of binders jam-packed with presentations and notes from these meetings. Low-hanging fruit—the good ideas that could be implemented quickly at low cost—were sometimes executed by phone before the end of the meeting.

Other ideas wound through the committee, board, and partner voting process before becoming company policy. The best ideas simply propagated themselves through positive gossip—the hotel bar served as the ultimate classroom/boardroom as managers, regional managers, KSC staff, and partners pitched, lobbied, and bragged their ideas into the imaginations of their friends. In Milwaukee, we also managed a remarkable mass karaoke version of "Under The Boardwalk." It was very hard to sell a mediocre idea to this group of frugal skeptics, but you couldn't stop a good idea from eventually spreading across the company.

One can debate whether "eventually" constitutes an acceptable timeframe for implementation of new ideas. We prioritized and executed essential policies such as cash-control procedures quickly and more uniformly than new products or production system modifications. The magic of our more organic method for spreading ideas around the company was the managers' and coworkers' opportunity to sell each other and buy in to an idea before adopting it.

Company Meetings

Partnerships held their own meetings and, over the years, I participated in gatherings of the Los Angeles area partners, Kinko's of Georgia (later Southeast Kinko's), Kinko's of Ohio, Salt Lake Kinko's, Kinko's of Arizona, K-Graphics, Kinko's Houston III, Kinko's Northwest, and many others.

The company meetings presented a microcosm of the larger organization, flavored by the personality of the partner. Some, like Kinko's Northwest, were examples of direct participatory democracy. Others were more like the mafia meetings you see in the movies. At one 1986 or 1987 gathering of the Los Angeles area partners, Dennis Itule sat quietly at the back of the room. As his partners and I discussed and debated an ad campaign I had proposed for the area, I noticed that every now and then a partner would turn to Denny, who would either nod or shake his head. Now, Dennis Itule is about the friendliest, sweetest guy you'll ever meet, but I saw that day why some of my more experienced coworkers referred to him as "the godfather." I mean that in the "quiet, influential benefactor" way; he was sharing his opinion, not making demands.

But at all the company meetings I attended, regardless of the education, experience, or management style of the partner, open communication ruled. Maybe staff people like me simply weren't invited to partnerships that operated otherwise. I don't know, but the companies I visited represented the vast majority of stores. KSC Operations VP Karen Madden once accused me of relishing debate for the sake of debate. Perhaps that's true, but if so, I had come to the right place. At the company meetings, people were in their ultimate cocoon of family safety and eagerly expressed their opinions.

Store Meetings

Because I spent most of my career on the road, I attended hundreds of store meetings. Some were run better than others, but only the least able managers prevented coworkers from speaking up and taking ownership in the quality of their store. Over a lengthy career, Carl Moyer was a key operator, delivery driver, manager, and regional trainer for Kinko's of Eugene and Kinko's Northwest. Here's his take on store meetings:

The Coworker's Voice

The thing I liked best about store meetings was that everyone was expected to come, and we worked hard to make sure our entire staff could be there. We got coverage from other stores and brought lots of good pizza. Everyone felt like part of the team. I remember my first meeting in Eugene, not knowing everyone and feeling out of place. When most of the group went out for beer after the meeting, I felt much more welcome. Funny how beer does that.

The best (unintended?) outcome of store meetings was covering other branch's meetings. At Tukwila we needed twice the coverage that other stores needed, so we'd have to trade with two other branches for staff. That meant that the leadership group (typically) spent a few hours every month in two other branches. And there was generally something that we saw that we stole and put into place back in Tukwila. I'd imagine that, consciously or not, that was a great source of best practice sharing.

Carl Moyer, Manager, Tukwila, Washington

Carl went on to say, "The big down side was a lack of meeting skills. The majority of meetings I went to (and led) didn't have agendas and the time wasn't truly well used. Typically, it was just a scattershot of hot issues." To solve this, Kinko's Northwest Regional Trainer Kelly Anderson wrote a "Meeting Management for Dummies" booklet with tips, tricks, and techniques for more effective meetings.

E Pluribus Kinko's

Friday Meetings @ KSC

I don't know how long the tradition continued, but when I was at KSC in 1986, we gathered the entire company on Friday mornings to hear from the President, Department VPs, and pretty much anyone who had something to say. It was a nice way to make personal contact with people from other departments. At one of my first meetings, I noticed a trash can full of paper clips and complained that someone was throwing away profits that would buy me a Ferrari one day. For years afterward, coworkers would ask whether I'd gotten my Ferrari yet. I didn't mind the teasing, because I had a like-minded comrade; I remember Paul leaving a VMX thirteen years later, lambasting coworkers for using FedEx when standard mail would suffice. Seems ironic now, as FedEx prepares to remove the Kinko's name from the stores.

All these meetings must have some of you rolling your eyes, wondering when we got any work done. But profit generation and problem solving *was* our work, and all these meetings helped us build relationships that advanced our goals. We got to meet people in positions very different from our own, broadening our understanding of the company. Actually, Paul and I shared a common enthusiasm for inter-departmental communications. That's why, even though neither of us were smokers, we would usually bum a cigarette to join a store or office's smokers on a break. The smokers' ghetto seems to be the one place in every organization where people from different departments get together regularly and without defensive postures.

Dean Zatkowsky

Kinko's University

If the best way to predict the future is to create the future, Kinko's University may have been the most effective expression of coworker participation as a key success factor.

Because Kinko's grew up around college campuses, we had a natural attraction to the higher education environment, yet many of our partners and regional managers had not completed college—sometimes because they were making too much money at Kinko's. Kinko's University gave us a taste of business school, tailored to our own business. And true to Paul Orfalea's *modus operandi*, the school provided another forum for disrupting our complacency.

Kinko's university disrupted complacency by challenging partners and regional managers with new ideas in leadership and management. In the classroom, the company's key decision-makers learned a common language that improved communication and made debates more practical. To this day, when I mention the Skylab case study, the Four Competencies, or the Strawberries article to former colleagues, they know exactly what I'm talking about.

We invited business professors from USC, Harvard, and other elite institutions to lead us in case studies and problem solving exercises. We held sessions at schools like USC, UCSB, and Arizona State, but also at posh resorts like Pinehurst in North Carolina.

Being the bookish type, I enjoyed the case studies and group projects. But everybody enjoyed another educational tradition: Dr. John Davis used feature films to lead discussions on situational leadership, the four competencies of leadership, teambuilding, etc. He showed films like *Hoosiers* and *Stand and Deliver*, pausing every half hour or so to discuss the management principles presented in the drama. To this day, if I stumble onto *Stand and Deliver* while channel surfing, when Edward James Olmos dons a fast-food paper hat and violently chops an onion in his math classroom, I reflexively blurt out, "The first competency of leadership is managing attention."

The Coworker's Voice

At Kinko's University, everyone was a peer. There was no difference between the biggest partner and the smallest—everyone was a student. Project groups were purposely divided into people from different locations and different positions. We liked to mix it up.

Karen Madden, Operations VP, Kinko's Service Corporation

Dean Zatkowsky

The Picnic

"The Picnic is No Picnic," said the signs adorning the wall of the Marketing department in May 1986. For Kinko's Service Corporation coworkers, the picnic was indeed no picnic, as we played host to first hundreds and eventually thousands of Kinko's managers, regional managers, partners, vendors, and partnership office staff.

The Picnic included a vendor show, educational workshops, and a comprehensive company meeting, but these played a secondary role to the picnic's true purpose: to provide a weeklong networking beer blast. We believed in the *in vino veritas* school of thought: give someone a couple of drinks and you'll learn what they really think. If so, the picnic must have been the candor center of the universe. Sure there was trouble, and even tragedy, but human liberty is troublesome and sometimes tragic.

I'm finding it difficult to write about the Picnic. You know how they say that if you can remember the 1960s, you weren't there? Our picnics had a bit of that 1960s vibe to them. It wasn't so much the drink and drugs, although there was plenty of that. I think it had a lot more to do with sleep deprivation. People working for the Service Corporation could find themselves working twenty-hour-days for weeks before, during, and after the Picnic. Those who lost sleep working were working to ensure others could lose sleep partying. We slept when we passed out.

Imagine a couple thousand overworked, overpaid, very energetic people taking over an entire resort for four or five days, with beer flowing 24/7, annual trysts celebrated, libidos unleashed, and limits explored. But wait, these were business meetings with classes, workshops, and presentations as well. We somehow managed to lose all of our behavioral moorings without abandoning any of the responsibilities of work. Instead, we funneled those shared pressures into shared release.

People who really knew how to work hard and play hard started the Kinko's Picnic: Brad and Stuie Krause. In 1971, they gathered their print shop coworkers at Santa Barbara's Skofield Park for hot dogs, burgers, Frisbees, etc. Paul loved the event and decided to make it an annual ritual for the whole company. As the Picnic grew, the organizers avoided metropolitan areas and opted instead for isolated resorts. I'm confident this kept a lot of coworkers out of jail.

By 1986 the Picnic was a big production with custom logos and themes, such as "Navigating New Directions." Whatever the official theme of the picnic, my friends and I always had our own theme: In addition to "The Picnic is No Picnic," there was "Squeal Like a Picnic" for our first visit to Lake of the Ozarks, Missouri. We called the post rollup 1998 San Diego Picnic, "Pink Slips at the Harbor."

On several occasions, I worked the Vendor Show, which was a giant trade show devoted entirely to products and services for our stores. Since I bookended my career at Kinko's Service Corporation and Kinko's Corporate Office, I worked the Marketing Booth at the beginning and end of my career. For the 1987 picnic, we created photographic masks of Paul's face, so that when he entered the Vendor Show, hundreds of Pauls were waiting for him. In 1998, I hosted Marketing Tool Time. My colleague, James Hilyard, built a magnificent set for me, using Kinko's giant color inkjet printers and mounting services. There was an eight-foot tall hammer, and a giant pair of pliers, etc., adorning my booth. I did my best Tim Allen impression and conducted presentations on how to use marketing tools from the corporate office.

The Coworker's Voice

The vendor show was a great way to learn that the branch mattered. There's nothing like professionals sucking up to us for a few hours to make us feel valued. To see the money our vendors spent to court MY opinion (in whatever thin slice) made me realize that my job function was important. To have the company fly me (as a 23-year-old for my first one) around the country reinforced that same thing. Picnic day itself was also a great message. Fun mattered, and our money was where our mouth was. I've never seen that kind of clarity since.

Carl Moyer, Manager, Tukwila, Washington

The Picnic brought EVERYONE together. We renewed commitments and observed traditions. Some of the traditions I enjoyed most included the talent show, which typically included company President Dan Frederickson belting out some badass rock and roll; the hospitality suite, which guaranteed that whenever my blood sugar tanked, I could find something to eat and some drunk friends to chat with; and the end-of-picnic slide show, displayed at the closing night party, of photos taken during the Picnic. The slide show was important because we did so much in three or four days, we needed photographic reminders of all the fun we had!

Another tradition I observed every year was my declaration: "This will be my last Picnic." This started in 1986, when Charley Williams ran us ragged at the Mandalay Bay Resort in Oxnard, California. Because I was the new guy, I was assigned to work the hospitality suite during the closing night party, the end of Picnic sybaritic celebration. Others might have seen this as a drag, but I was grateful for the break, knowing I would have no guests to serve during the big party. I was on duty with Rod Tryon, KSC graphic artist and all-around good guy. There was one kid playing pool. Otherwise, we had the cold cuts and beer kegs to ourselves, finally getting a break after weeks of continuous work.

Then, I heard a commotion. Moving to the doorway, I saw a long line of stumbling, staggering, half-dancing people headed my way, drunkenly chattering and laughing. Apparently, the party got so wild, with so many people dancing, that the newly built Mandalay Bay Resort feared for the safety of their building—the chandelier downstairs was shaking too dangerously for their liking. So they shut down the party and the revelers descended—by the hundreds—on the hospitality suite where Rod and I had been relaxing. "Never again," I promised myself in vain.

Being socially inept and an incompetent drinker, I found Picnics extremely stressful. While others partied, I usually had to prepare presentations or clean up after sloppy drunks or spend late night hours staring at my wedding ring for strength. I almost never attended Picnic Day, because that was one event where I had no responsibilities, and by then I was fed up with the whole deal.

Even so, I concede that my happiest Kinko's memory is picnic-related. In Nashville, two Regional Managers (Jim Downey and John Odell), two store managers (Sorry, I can't remember your names), and I found that we had a free day. Or maybe we played hooky. But we went guitar shopping. We visited legendary shops like Gruhn Guitars and Cotton Music Center, and we visited pawnshops. And between each shop, we visited bars to have a beer and talk guitars. We talked about instruments we'd love to play and the ones that got away. We walked into one pawnshop and stopped dead at the sight of an ancient, blonde Fender Vibrolux amplifier, covered with beer stains and cigarette burns. The proprietor let his own cigarette dangle from his lips as he announced to us in a slow, magnificent drawl, and with considerable pride, "That's one dirty dawg." When New Orleans Regional Manager John Odell played through that amp, we understood completely. Beer, guitars, and friends in Music City. I was so happy.

Mike Fasth says the Picnic captured the essence of his Kinko's memories: "It was fun and we had friends." And as I like to point out, people will work very hard for their friends.

E Pluribus Kinko's

The Newsletter

Internal company newsletters are notorious for causing so much eye-rolling that coworkers risk serious ocular injury. Former Operations VP Karen Madden read an early draft of this book and pointed out something I had overlooked: coworkers seemed to genuinely enjoy the Kinko's Newsletter. Not only did coworkers regularly talk to me about articles, but many of them also contributed to the newsletter.

Like many company newsletters, our Newsletter was a vehicle for rah-rah propaganda, but it also offered useful company statistics (how did your color copy sales compare with national averages?), helpful hints from peers (how to clean flooring tiles, or how to psychologically prepare your Xerox technician for the 2.5¢ Sale), and genuine controversy, as field coworkers and office staff debated advertising strategies or departmental performance.

Many companies struggle to produce a monthly two-page newsletter. We struggled to keep ours under sixteen pages. It included feature stories, coworker recognition, store records, letters to the editor, etc. While at KSC, I did some newsletter ghostwriting for Paul's column; thus began our twenty-three-plus-year writing collaboration. We wanted the Newsletter to foster dialogue between KSC and the field, but we learned through trial-and-error that personal catfights diminished the value of debate. Yes, it was me. Soon after I left KSC, I took potshots at the Marketing Department through letters to the editor, and the VP of Marketing responded in kind. It was not the finest hour for either of us.

Eventually, the pendulum swung too far from the Newsletter's original open forum. When I wrote a letter describing Seattle Manager Juli Ulvestad's Jedi Mind Tricks sales technique,* the editor refused to run the story, because she feared George Lucas would sue us. This is what happens when companies start to take themselves too seriously.

Part of what made the Newsletter useful to coworkers also made it useful to competitors, so the company eventually became paranoid about confidentiality. This diminished the publication's effectiveness because stores removed it from the bathroom. Here's some free advice: if you want coworkers to read your newsletter, write short articles, print it on paper, and keep copies in the bathroom. PDF newsletters are easy to ignore and too difficult to bring into the primary reading room.

The last article I remember contributing to the Newsletter I wrote while waiting in an airplane on the tarmac at JFK airport in New York. Reflecting on my customer service experiences as a frequent traveler and thinking about how large Kinko's had grown, I reminded coworkers of the butterfly effect. We served over half a million customers each day and I wanted coworkers to consider that the kindness they shared with customers would surely ripple outward to the customer's family, friends, and coworkers. So would our indifference. A kind word at the right moment might later prevent someone from kicking a dog—or a child.

In combination with our voicemail system, the Newsletter was part of our pre-Internet social networking system, and was just as addictive for some people as Facebook and email are today.

*Juli and I firmly believed that the customer is the only true judge of quality, but the customer doesn't always know what's possible or even what they want. Many of our coworkers were artists and very proud of their skill in producing

E Pluribus Kinko's

top quality copies and prints, but color can be a very personal thing. Often I saw coworkers approaching the counter with a color copy, and just before the customer could say, "Wow, that looks great!" the coworker would frown, say something like, "Oh, the green is a little off," and turn around to try again—instantly doubling the supplies cost. Juli showed her coworkers that, if you handed a print to the customer while saying, "It looks great," the customer would take the print, study it, and in a voice like a Star Wars storm trooper, reply, "Yes, this looks great." They depended on us to be the experts.

KVMX: The Power of the Human Voice

In 1988, Kinko's Service Corporation, Kinko's Northwest, and Kinko's of Georgia moved into an expansive, two-story office building in Ventura, California. Prior to the move, at 4141 State Street in Santa Barbara, a receptionist answered phones and wrote down messages in those two-part NCR message books, later distributing the message slips to coworker mailboxes. In Ventura, we got a phone system with voicemail. Stemming in part from our leader's dyslexia, Kinko's had always leaned toward the oral tradition. Voicemail allowed us to communicate in many of the great ways email would later provide: We could leave messages for individuals without interrupting them, letting them respond at their convenience. We could send out mass messages (for better or worse) and receive personal or public responses. Voicemail brought a new immediacy to coworker participation.

And to Paul's delight, voicemail allowed us to debate issues between gatherings. I'm sure it drove a lot of people crazy, but wherever Paul happened to be, if he encountered someone with an idea he wanted to share, he would call into the system, shove his phone into the face of the coworker, vendor, or complete stranger, and thousands of us would hear what they had to say. And we responded.

The KVMX system, as we called it, let us tailor conversations to the way we worked. For example, one morning, as I was about to depart from the Santa Barbara airport, I left a message for the Kinko's Northwest managers, asking what techniques they used for mitigating coworker stress. When I changed planes in San Francisco, I checked my messages and had fifty-five responses. Some I forwarded immediately because they were brilliant or funny (like the coworkers of San Rafael fishing in the creek behind the store), and the others I shared in the course of my job, spreading positive gossip store-to-store.

A hyperactive dyslexic with an antipathy toward complacency could not ask for a better weapon than the company-wide voicemail system. Some might consider Paul's use of voicemail analogous to Big Brother's video screen or Tokyo Rose's radio transmissions; it allowed Paul to be present in every store, partnership, and regional office, delivering his personal propaganda every day, if he so chose. Paul would sometimes use it to needle those who had been slow to adopt new services: "Only do this if you want to make money," he would say, or "Hey, pussycats, I don't want to be a pussycat anymore." We knew he wasn't calling us cats. With this amazing tool, Paul could engage in his favorite activity from anywhere at any time: he could lob a stink bomb right into the middle of the company. And believe it or not, those stink bombs were another key success factor.

SECTION 4: BOY AND BUSINESS QUARREL

Pot Stirring

Attention Deficit Dynamic

Edward Abbey said, "Society is like a stew. If you don't stir it up every now and then, a layer of scum floats to the top."

I was on the phone, trying to schedule lunch with a Regional Manager visiting from Texas. I told her I couldn't make plans for Tuesday, because I expected a visit from Paul. She laughed and said, "I've never had someone tell me so calmly that a tornado is heading his way."

Paul Orfalea had an interesting way of staying relevant to coworkers: he caused a lot of trouble. However much his friends may enjoy Paul's company, most of us can only take his high-energy and sudden mood swings in small doses. He asks a lot of questions and challenges the answers. It took me years to get over the feeling that I was constantly being tested. Oh wait, I still haven't gotten over that feeling. But that's just who he is. He likes to know what people think and he likes to keep things moving. He cannot sit still and seems suspicious of anyone who can.

E Pluribus Kinko's

Part of Paul's pot-stirring aptitude can be attributed to his ADHD; he needs constant stimulation and constant challenges, so when things seem a little too quiet, he creates his own disruptions. But Paul's eternal campaign against complacency springs less from a short attention span than from a multi-generational business sensibility. He believes that entrepreneurship makes you free, but the price of freedom is eternal vigilance. As Benjamin Franklin, another man who made his fortune with partnership print shops, put it, "The eye of the master will do more work than both his hands." Of course, if the master sticks his nose into everything, it can get pretty annoying.

Paul absolutely detests "analysis paralysis." Once, while visiting the Sahara Pavilion store in Las Vegas, Paul leapt atop the front counter to get the attention of customers. He wanted their opinion on where to hang a new sign. He moved from place-to-place, holding up the sign and getting customer reactions. With this quick and simple *action*, Paul showed his coworkers how a "just try it" attitude and a partnership ethos—involving customers and coworkers in the decision—made the decision easier and more fun. It also strengthened the bond between coworkers and customers.

Some people dismiss the following as hyperbole, but it's an honest-to-goodness fact: some time after the company rollup facilitated by Clayton, Dubilier and Rice, Kinko's founder Paul Orfalea was banned from his own office building. People who knew Paul's history of volatility were not surprised. Paul raged through our offices in Ventura, decrying bureaucracy and waste. Part of it was genuine frustration; part of it was theater.

Dean Zatkowsky

The Coworker's Voice

Whatever Paul's reputation in public, I know him as the guy who would come into my office, close the door, and grill me on ways we could pay more for coworkers' families' insurance.

Jack Woodruff, Controller, Kinko's Service Corporation

Paul liked to fight waste, but he also liked to fight "the man." Unfortunately, Paul saw any authority figure as "the man" sooner or later. In *Copy This*, Dan Frederickson described the situation from his point of view as president of the company from 1986–1996. The partners hired Dan to bring order to the chaos of our organization, and he took this responsibility seriously, but the deck was stacked against him:

Paul could be abusive. He's immature. He could be hostile. But he could flip that and be phenomenally gracious. He would create chaos. There was constant turmoil in the organization. You never knew what was expected of you. Paul's extremely difficult to work with because everything is so personal. It was very hard on me, especially in the long run. Some of the partners thought the most important thing in the world was to manage him. You look at the stress I put myself through personally. I definitely would have taken the job, but I would have gotten out earlier. As for the company, it was a very in-your-face culture. The partners were very independent. They felt they owned the business and no one could tell them what to do.

(In one interview for this book, Operations VP Karen Madden pointed out the irony of this last statement: It wasn't just a feeling—the partners DID own the business.)

E Pluribus Kinko's

For better or worse, Paul set the example. When Dan first arrived at KSC, he wore suits, as he had at Xerox. A few days after he settled into his new office (adjacent to—and facing—the building's main bathroom, so that Dan learned far more about his coworkers than he ever wanted), a young woman barely covered in ratty jeans and a cropped top strode into his office, pointed angrily at him and said, "You're making me uncomfortable." Nothing at Xerox or in the Marine Corps could have prepared Dan for Kinko's culture.

Although Dan and I were hired within days of one another, I never worked closely with him and did not know him well. Instead of getting to know him as a person, I viewed him as a symbol of top-down management. When I think about the stress-inducing chaos of 1986–1996, which Dan and I obviously saw from different perspectives (by 1988, I was ensconced in one of those partnerships where the people didn't want to be told what to do), I note that these were the GOLDEN YEARS of growth and profitability. So I believe there was a great value to Paul's pot stirring, but I recognize that balancing the mayhem took a personal toll on many in the company.

Since I held positions in a partnership and at the corporate level, I'd like to clarify one portion of Dan's statement: I think it's absolutely correct that at Kinko's Service Corporation "you never knew what was expected of you." Paul hated overhead and had trouble seeing offices as anything but. So he did not mind that partnerships peppered KSC with continuous, and often conflicting, demands. As a marketing manager for Kinko's Northwest, however, I knew exactly what was expected of me, and so did everyone in our office: We were expected to make the stores more profitable—in perpetuity, if possible.

Paul's personal pot stirring set an example that many others followed, to Dan's chagrin. I feel bad about how difficult it must have been for Dan, but I see three aspects of the company's culture that made the nurturing of chaos work so well for us:

1) As a **Private** company, we were free from outside pressures that might have limited candor and forced a less democratic structure onto the organization.

2) The **Pendulum** of power swung constantly between the field and the home office, and we often talked about "states' rights vs. federalism." A messy democracy tends to be far more innovative than an orderly tyranny. While we wrestled with company-wide decisions, stores profited from their own micro-innovations. For *this* location, with *this* furniture, *these* machines, and *these* customers, what is the best way to layout the self-service area? Only the local coworkers know for sure, so when the pendulum swung toward the stores, pluralism created a thousand unique *permutations* of the Kinko's ideal.

3) **Playfulness** was an essential element; without it, the contentiousness and candor we so valued would degrade relationships and prevent teamwork. One coworker described the Picnic as "the end-of-term dorm party where rivals drink heavily and declare all is forgiven."

Let's take a look at these three attributes in greater detail.

Public Conflict in a Private Company

Before we started renting computers by the hour, people didn't spend much time in a Kinko's store unless they worked there. In 1985, I needed three copies of a screenplay, so I went to the Kinko's at 4141 State Street in Santa Barbara. The woman at the counter asked if I wanted to wait, which I thought was an absurd question; I believed it would take hours to make three copies of 120 pages, because that's how long it would have taken on the dime machine over at Thrifty's. I dropped off the script and drove straight home, where a message on my answering machine said the copies were ready. Kinko's was all about speed in those days and I was duly impressed.

Two years later, when I was a Kinko's coworker and my dad needed passport photos, I took him to the Huntington Beach, California Kinko's. After Dad bought his pictures, I got involved in a conversation with the manager, so my dad stood nearby and watched the cash register for about fifteen minutes. On the way home, he said, "That cash register

E Pluribus Kinko's

never took a break. There was never a long line, but there was always a line. They just kept handing over their money." In those few minutes, my dad saw what most people had not: Kinko's was doing great business, one nickel at a time. Like a fast food restaurant, we focused on getting the jobs—and the customers—in-and-out as quickly as possible.

We liked the fact that most people thought we were a little local shop. When my dad wore a Kinko's sweatshirt to Disneyland one day, dozens of people from all over the country thought he was from their hometown, because that's where Kinko's was. At the time, this misunderstanding was part of our competitive advantage—we didn't look like a threat to anyone.

If you don't need a lot of capital right away, there are many reasons for remaining a private company, but chief among them is privacy. Because we didn't have to publish our figures, and because no one believed a multi-billion dollar company could be built on nickel transactions, Kinko's was able to operate under the radar just long enough to become an 800-pound gorilla in the quick-print business. By the time our larger competitors took us seriously, there was nothing they could do about us.

Anyone who pays attention can quickly figure out a company's strengths and weaknesses. But most people don't pay attention. They rely on their ears instead of their eyes. That's why Paul says that when business is good, you should complain, but when business is bad, you should brag. Many people believe your words and never notice whether customers are lining up to give you money.

The major disadvantage of our status as a private company was our dependence on cash flow. When the company derived most of its income from Professor Publishing and other campus-related sales, we faced tremendous cash crises every summer and every December. Our sales chart looked like the Golden Gate Bridge, with a couple of huge peaks holding the whole thing together. By 1988, however, those peaks were big enough to subsidize our move to the suburbs and downtown districts, which proved lifesaving when we had to shut down the Professor Publishing business. We still had peaks and valleys, but the valleys were less deep every year.

One counterintuitive advantage of our status as a private company was the luxury of airing our dirty laundry as publicly as we wanted. We wrestled and argued and threw tantrums right there in our Newsletter. Unlike public companies, we did not have to beg forgiveness from cold-hearted institutional investors when an experimental product or service didn't work out. We allowed ourselves to fail, forgave ourselves and moved forward. "Fail Fast" is one of those *In Search of Excellence* lessons that just seems a lot easier to implement in a private company, presuming the leadership desires creativity, innovation, and loyalty.

The Coworker's Voice

I don't remember seeking conflict, but we weren't afraid of it, either. Within the branch, my success came from listening to the coworkers. That's where I learned I worked for them—I largely just needed to do what they suggested to succeed. Many brains made light work. Ideas bubbled up from the front line better at Kinko's than anyplace I've ever seen.

Carl Moyer, Manager, Tukwila, Washington

Yet another advantage of Kinko's network of private, limited partnerships was the fact that coworkers generally knew the people signing their paychecks.

The Coworker's Voice

My coworkers and I would go to the Santa Barbara Air Show, where Brad Krause would be doing an exhibition race, and before the race, we'd hang out with them; I played Frisbee with Brad's dog. And I was just a front-line kind of guy. Having personal interaction with the guys I knew were profiting most from my work made it a lot easier for me to do that work. These weren't abstract, distant people in their ivory towers. They were MY coworkers, too; these were the people who created something powerful, which was the entire reason I was employed.

Tom Hudson, Coworker, Santa Barbara, California

During my first visit to Seattle, there were five Pauls working in the area, including Regional Manager Peggy VanWaard's husband. But at a meeting of managers and assistant managers that included all five Pauls, I observed that whenever someone referred to "Paul," everyone in the room knew exactly who was being discussed: Paul Orfalea. For years I debated whether this was a good thing or a bad thing, because as my friend, John Huffman, once pointed out, it seemed as if the company were structured to self-destruct upon Paul's departure. But when I interviewed Mike Fasth about Kinko's key success factors, he felt there was tremendous power in the fact that everyone in the company knew the owner. That feeling of direct communication built loyalty and engagement, even when there were 25,000 of us.

Paul saw himself as the company mascot and spent as much time as possible in the field. Coworkers all over the country knew Kinko himself. At the Picnic, he greeted them upon arrival and saw them off at the end. People got very excited when Paul visited their stores, not in fear of the boss, but because they liked him and wanted to impress him. Steve Astrich managed a Kinko's store in Houston for years and now owns his own shop, staffed with many former Kinkoids. While researching this book, I got in touch with Steve and we exchanged some emails. He sent his regards to Paul and invited him to visit the store. Steve discussed the hypothetical visit with one of his coworkers, who exclaimed, "We've got to do some cleaning!" This was thirteen years after these two had left Kinko's.

The Coworker's Voice

I worked for Kinko's from 1991-2004 and my husband worked there from 1992—1996. Just a few months ago, I was flipping channels at about 2:00 a.m. and caught a replay of one of Paul's talks on C-Span. Woke my husband up and we both watched it until 3:00 a.m. We loved hearing him again.

E Pluribus Kinko's

And, as a fellow dyslexic, I have to say he has provided a lot of inspiration to me. That, and the whole story of how Kinko's evolved, and the stories the partners tell from the early days, has inspired many coworkers to strive for their dreams.

Carrie Gaddess Mudge, Assistant Manager,
Birmingham, Michigan

When the company started looking for a way to go public, Paul and I had a few animated voicemail conversations about the concept of ownership. As I've mentioned, the partnership structure was becoming unwieldy; Paul and his existing partners had no exit plan and he felt that going public would give coworkers a greater opportunity for an ownership stake. Naturally, I disagreed and waxed melodramatic, asking which provided a greater sense of ownership, a few shares of stock or a feeling of autonomy?

There was no doubt in my mind that once we chose the path of going public—whether or not we achieved an IPO—we would lose the sense of self-determination and independence that had made Kinko's so attractive to talented people. It got tougher as we grew, but even when we had a thousand stores and 25,000 coworkers, anyone in the company could easily get in touch with their store's owner. How many public companies of any size can say that?

Dean Zatkowsky

The Coworker's Voice

Well, a guy I worked with in Columbia, Missouri told me a story. This happened a couple weeks before I started in Columbia in 1995. Paul came with a group of execs. When they came in the door, the execs all headed back to the back to talk with the store manager, while Paul grabbed the nearest co-worker (this guy in dreadlocks), and asked where the nearest vending machine was.

The co-worker took him to the bank next door where there was a machine. He found Paul to be a complete opposite of the "suits" that accompanied him, and that there appeared to be a little discord there. He said Paul seemed much more willing to talk with the co-workers than the managers. The suits? They completely ignored the co-workers.

Kevin Gabbert, Coworker, Missouri

The Power Pendulum

Independence mattered to partners and managers because they understood the intimate details of their stores and had a very personal stake in the outcome. And that personal involvement made our debates very fierce. As I mentioned earlier, I spent two years at KSC, then joined Kinko's Northwest for eight years, stayed with Brad Krause for two years at Kinko's Western Division after the company rollup, and finished my career back at the central organization, then called Kinko's Corporate Office.

After the Service Corporation was created, it seemed that every idea, regardless of its source, turned into a power struggle between the field and "corporate." The power pendulum swung back and forth during my time at Kinko's, creating rivalries and outright feuds. As both a partner and president of the Service Corporation, Dan was right in the middle of every conflict. He told me, "Friction made the end product better, but it was horribly painful for a lot of people." As the pendulum swung toward the stores, innovation

E Pluribus Kinko's

and experimentation flourished. When the pendulum swung toward the Service Corporation, we tried to select and implement best practices from those experiments. It was an extremely messy process, but we licked our wounds and moved on to the next battle.

Among "States' Rights" managers, Dan was the bad cop and Paul was the good cop, but back at KSC, those roles were reversed. Paul raged through the building, decrying bureaucracy and perceived waste. Word leaked out, enhancing his legend in the field. I think a lot of this was PR, because Paul was just as obsessed with Dan when it came to implementing best practices. But Paul led through the force of his personality, whereas Dan led through salesmanship, in the best sense of the word.

Both of these strong leaders played essential roles in the growth of Kinko's, yet I've come to see them as secondary to a much greater force: an army of highly motivated, anonymous twenty-somethings who poured themselves into their work, executing the mundane details of the business, learning how to diagnose a jammed Xerox 9500 through the laying on of hands, deciding to clean and organize the storeroom because they were bored, inventing custom calendars or workarounds for getting cardstock through a printer not designed for it. At the store level, there was this electrifying sense of camaraderie and collaborative competition.

I don't like to read too much into semantics, but the names we applied expressed our ambivalence toward centralized power. Kinko's Service Corporation was supposed to provide services to the stores, not policy. When I joined

Kinko's Northwest as Marketing Director, I got a desk at the "Home Office."

"Home office" always reminded me of George Carlin's routine about the semantics of football versus baseball:

In football the object is for the quarterback, also known as the field general, to be on target with his aerial assault, riddling the defense by hitting his receivers with deadly accuracy in spite of the blitz, even if he has to use a shotgun. With short bullet passes and long bombs, he marches his troops into enemy territory, balancing this aerial assault with a sustained ground attack that punches holes in the forward wall of the enemy's defensive line.

In baseball the object is to go home! And to be safe!—I hope I'll be safe at home!

Why wouldn't a family business have a home office? One of the strengths of Kinko's original partnership model was the fact that, even when we had 126 partners and over 1,000 stores, we continued to operate like small businesses in our communities. The passion and connectedness of local involvement was good for the coworkers, good for the business, and good for the communities we served.

Efficiency versus Effectiveness

So when the pendulum swung between KSC and the field, it usually swung between calls for greater consistency and demands for independence. I understood the problem very well, because when I was at KSC, I wanted greater consistency in the field, and when I was in the field, I wanted complete independence to make local, market-specific decisions. In both cases, I thought that what was best for the company would be whatever made my job easier.

As usual, the pot-stirrer-in-chief was part of the problem. Visiting coworkers in stores or offices, Paul constantly asked, "How can I make your job easier?" I came to believe that was the wrong question, because I'd rather know what coworkers needed to be more effective. At least then they would have to think about what it meant to be effective. Instead, Paul promoted the idea that everyone should be thinking about how to make his or her job easier. Many lost sight of a more important question: what is my job?

I often rant that consistency and efficiency are false idols. As the Marketing, Operations, Finance, and IT departments grew, so did the reflexive demands for greater efficiency. At KSC, efficiency was equated with consistency. At the store level, efficiency meant, "whatever works." Granted, provincialism sometimes prevailed over practicality, but no amount of store-level recalcitrance was likely to damage the overall company.

KSC coworkers used to freak out when a customer complained that he or she could not, for example, get the exact same paper in Stockton, California and New York City, but seriously, folks, when the presence of Kinko's meant the difference between having your presentation or not having your presentation, did a cover letter on linen versus laid paper really make or break the deal? I concede that this may have been very important to some of our customers, but trying to please everybody can be dangerous, and I don't think we fully appreciated the cultural and economic consequences of demanding store-to-store conformity.

Paul played both sides. When he saw something he liked, he insisted, "What's good for the goose is good for the gander," and, therefore, everybody should adopt the new product, service, or policy. But when coworkers in the field complained about top-down mandates, he railed against the demands of KSC and the partnership offices. Sure, this drove some people crazy, but keeping that power pendulum swinging brought tremendous energy to the organization. What he wanted most was engagement.

The Coworker's Voice

Paul would rant, but it was a display of passion for his company, wanting people to think. Not that it's the most effective management style, but I remember one day he was cruising through and saw a stack of FedEx letters ready to ship out. Many of them were to the same address. He was incensed because it was a waste of money—why didn't they group the same addresses together and send one big package? He spent the entire afternoon going from department to department to get the answer he wanted to hear ... that it WAS the wrong procedure and that we realized it and would change it. He wanted us to LEARN.

Joanna Murphy, Marketing Department, Kinko's Service Corporation

Our paradoxical support for both decentralized power and centralized authority created manageable controversies that kept people philosophically engaged in the business, debating interesting questions. For example, if we're in the creativity business, should the Santa Cruz, California, and Ames, Iowa, stores be the same? But, wait a minute; are we

E Pluribus Kinko's

in the creativity business? Shouldn't a business services provider offer the comfort of conformity for harried, traveling executives? Was Kinko's a thousand entrepreneurial retail stores or a thousand branches of the same company? Could it be both?

Permutations & Pluralism—In Ideas We Trust

The Coworker's Voice

I really appreciated the culture of allowing experimentation and mistakes. I worked up from the counter to store manager in the late '80s, and back then, I think there was a real feeling that this was such a new thing that we were all feeling our way forward—typically dealing with high growth, new technology, crazy customer expectations, all being run by a bunch of twenty-something philosophy majors. So much of what came to define the company came from individual stores trying new things and sharing successes.

Another thing I remember was the 2.5¢ sales. We did these for a week each summer until the early '90s I think. It was absolutely crazy. Lines at the self-service machines, pulling double and triple shifts, Xerox repair guys on-site all day with their shirttails hanging out, and all at an absolute loss financially. But there were a couple of huge payoffs. We absolutely owned the mindspace in town—everyone knew us. And we also proved to ourselves how much we could hustle; it really sharpened the Manager and Assistant Managers.

We spun on a dime when we finally had to get out of Professor Publishing. I remember the punch in the gut feeling when we got the KVMX announcing we were going completely out of the course reader business—I had a campus store. But Paul and the partners and that spirit of experimentation and hustle all worked together so that we (my store at least, but I think the whole company) still made revenue and profit growth that same year, with a whole new focus on business customers.

I really think I got an invaluable education through these experiences; one I could not have gotten through any school program.

Jim Perry, Director of Training, Kinko's Inc.

One of the key success factors created by decentralized power was the *de facto* existence of 1,000 research and development laboratories spread across the country. With a 90%+ gross margin, mistakes cost little. With the brand centered around speed and availability, slight variations in products or dress codes or equipment did not matter to the customers at all.

When the first serious color copiers arrived in stores, Kinko's Northwest put one in Pleasant Hill, California, and one in Portland, Oregon. We also tested them in other locations, but these were the two stores I visited shortly after the machines arrived. In one of the stores, the manager was very excited about the machine and the opportunity to test it. The other manager thought the machine produced poor quality prints (by today's standards this is unquestionably true, but at the time it was about as good as one could expect). As you can imagine, one store sold a lot of color copies and the other did not. This taught me two things: 1) any product gets a sales boost from enthusiasm, and 2) Kinko's was very lucky to be able to test products in a wide variety of circumstances. Better still, Kinko's was lucky to have coworkers who dared to experiment on their own. This is why, while we were still trying to figure out whether color copiers could be profitable and which machine we would prefer, a store in San Diego figured out how to make beautiful customized full color calendars from customer photographs.

The Coworker's Voice

As a campus store, we always struggled with the feast and famine seasonality of Professor Publishing. At the beginning of the each semester, Professor Publishing was an all-consuming, 24 hours a day, seven days a week, all hands on deck responsibility. I had coworkers so dedicated that they slept on the floor in the office. It was all pizza and caffeine, toner and spiral binding dust. It was intense and chaotic, but we took money to the bank in shopping bags. The store made good money, the coworkers made good money (seriously good money for who we were and what we were doing).

The downside was summer in campus stores, when the volume dropped by as much as 80%, and most often the store lost money. When the next semester came around, the store was in a profit hole that had to be filled before we got paid again. In the mid-1980s Kinko's were primarily thought of as just a campus copy shop, so getting commercial business was tough. Out of somewhere, my campus rep Dave Stern and I came up with the idea of selling copier paper in bulk. We ordered paper by the pallet, so we got it cheap and had a pile of it. Why not sell it? It was before Office Max and Staples, so the copy paper was a high profit item for local stationary stores.

I worked on the Record Holder database and Dave hit the phones. His opening line was "Do you have a copier in your office?" If they said "yes," we sold paper; if they said "no," we sold copy services. It wasn't too long before we had to rent a mini-warehouse because we were ordering truckloads of paper instead of pallets. Bulk paper proved to be a great short-term "cash cow," offsetting the summer profit hole, and over the long term providing an entry into the commercial market that we'd never been able to penetrate.

That year, two "ideas" were recognized at the Picnic in Lake of the Ozarks, including ours. I was invited to speak (with my long hair, tuxedo jacket, and black jeans) at the company meeting about "Seeding an Idea," and I went home with a new Macintosh SE. I'm sure that exposure had a big influence on being nominated for a position on the Marketing Committee and a promotion to Regional Manager later that fall.

Jim Downey, Regional Manager, Kinko's Graphics Corporation

We credited various coworkers with the invention of successful products—such as Liz and Chip Stanzcak's custom-color calendars—but I'd bet that a customer inspired the original creation. Coworkers were remarkably creative about inventing products on the spot. You can say that Kinko's was a copy shop and that, on the surface, all of our products were the same. But every job was unique. We were mass customization workshops. Did you ever order the exact same thing twice at a Kinko's? Every order had the potential to tax a coworker's creativity and that became a point of pride. And we never hid the factory—our production happened right there in front of the customers.

The Coworker's Voice

I do think the core job function (keeping the glue table* clear) was some part of the magic. It was a challenging, fast paced puzzle that drove a gunslinger attitude. Are you good enough to handle the challenge? Have you paid your dues so that you can try? Can you handle the speed and the pressure of customers staring at you while running multiple machines? It wasn't a typical retail environment.

Perhaps the replicable key was that it was a peer environment. WE ran it, or felt like it—not 'management'. Once I got into management, I saw that was a peer environment also. Competition between stores (in Seattle) was fierce. And fun. A significant amount of that was enabled by how much information sharing there was. Having done other things since, I've come to realize how unusual it was that the branch management team got the full P&Ls. There was upper management, but it was pretty hands off—results were what mattered. The peer structure drove best practices.

Carl Moyer, Manager, Tukwila, Washington

* Author's note: The Glue Table anchored our Glue System production process. It was the portal between the front counter, where orders were taken, and the production area.

E Pluribus Kinko's

❖ ❖ ❖

Coworkers made everything happen, and that's why some of us "management types" turned David Packard's "management by walking around" into management by gossiping around. Yes, the Commitments to Communication include "I will not gossip," but that's a reference to malicious gossip. Traveling executives were in the business of spreading positive gossip. I traveled three days a week, moving branch-to-branch, sharing stories of hiring practices, successful promotions, or how this or that store raised its color copy average just by wondering how to raise their copy average (sometimes, attention creates improvement).

Most people are cursed with a pathological need for a single correct answer and inflict this neurosis on their coworkers. They don't want to reinvent the wheel because—wait for it—that's inefficient. But reinventing the wheel teaches people how to create their own solutions. Sure, a thousand Kinko's branches had many common problems, but why prevent them from creating unique solutions? Is efficiency more important than innovation? (The correct answer is "sometimes," but when it's not, it's a terrible trade).

For example, many managers sought the right answer to the puzzle of labor percentage. As in most businesses, payroll constituted the largest controllable expense in a Kinko's store. Many Partners and Regional Managers set a specific number—for example, 21%. Kinko's Northwest Regional Manager Tom Parrish took a different approach, because he hired his managers to manage and trusted them to do so. Tom's elegant solution was the simple request that his managers ensure labor percentage was lower than profit percentage. He didn't set the numbers, just a goal that served everyone. He also managed the most profitable region in Kinko's Northwest.

But an approach like Tom's requires comfort with ambiguity and I think you'll find that proponents of centralized authority despise ambiguity. Over the years, as the power pendulum swung back and forth between Corporate and The Field, it generated friction. Dan Frederickson said the friction usually improved the end product, but it created quite a bit of heat as well. As in any large organization, rivalries and outright hatreds developed. I myself never got over my distrust of the corporate office as it grew ever larger and more detached from The Field. At the same time, many of my coworkers at Kinko's Northwest never got over my lack of "operations" experience.

As I've mentioned, being a private company allowed us to engage in very public squabbles, and many of us fought passionately for our individual points of view. What made this contentiousness a key success factor rather than a coffin nail? Once again, the credit belongs to our pot-stirrer-in-chief. The Kinko's culture reflected Paul Orfalea's multifaceted personality. He can be highly competitive, quick to anger, and casually cruel. He is also kind, generous, and thoughtful. He is all business, but he is also the class clown. And one should never underestimate the power of a clown.

Playfulness

One day, Paul Orfalea, Brad Krause, Mike Fasth, Peggy VanWaard, and I drove from Seattle to Portland. We had recently added custom-printing desks to several stores, and Paul wanted to visit the competition at every opportunity, so we pretty much stopped every time we saw a strip mall with a print shop. Sometimes I would go into the shop first to scout a little bit. Then Paul and Peggy would come in, pretending to be fiancés in need of wedding announcements. Their act was ludicrous: "What do you think, sweetie-cakes?" "Oh, I don't know, big boy, I need you to make these kind of decisions." They portrayed different characters at each stop and I couldn't stay in the shops for fear of lapsing into outright, prolonged laughter. My attempts to stifle my giggles usually earned ruder looks from the print shop employees than did Paul and Peggy's silliness.

Back in the car, Paul and Peggy reenacted their performances for the others and we laughed our heads off. But we also took notes. By the time we reached our destination, we knew who was offering truly custom printing, who used templates from outsource printers, and how much everybody charged for invitations, announcements, business cards, etc. We had a lot of fun and profited from it. Playfulness—in the service of business—describes the Kinko's culture as well as any other key success factor. Remember Mark Madden's four-word credo: "Have fun, make money."

Paul knew that fun was a big selling point for coworkers, and the company started in college towns, where education forms a thin veneer of respectability over a world of reckless, hedonistic abandon. As a hyperactive dyslexic, Paul always had a rough time in school, so his mom had to sell him on going to college, which she knew would be essential to his success in life. (Paul notes that in the late sixties, college was also the best alternative to a long-term camping excursion in Vietnam). His mom didn't try to pitch the value of college to his future; she just showed him the kids cavorting on campus and said, "Doesn't that look like fun?" Fun sells. And fun effectively balances the stress of a highly competitive, highly contentious environment. We didn't have to force the fun at Kinko's—we just tried to stay out of its way.

The Coworker's Voice

As I look back on my time at Kinko's, my dominant memory is my relationships with so many people. There were very few people that I disliked and there are many that I would call good friends. With as many hours that we spend at work, it's great to be at a place with people you enjoy. A second thought is that, being gone for a while, I tend to remember the fun. The reality is that we all worked real hard ... it wasn't easy ... but we had a good time

Dean Zatkowsky

doing it because the company was successful and we were generally working with friends.

Eric Schwarz, Finance VP, Kinko's Graphics Corporation

Cultures are built on stories; corporate cultures are no exception. Talk to any Kinko's coworker from any pre-rollup partnership and you will hear tales of food fights, trysts, jam sessions, dance marathons, stoned collating parties, etc. We used to brag about hotels and restaurants at which we were no longer welcome. (On the flip side, Dan Frederickson tells me that the staff at Tan-Tar-A resort in Missouri still talks about how well we treated them during the picnics held there.)

At the word "picnic," images flash into my mind: participants in the 5K race running with a beer keg on a stolen bellman's cart. At a 5K in San Diego, I distinctly remember handing out cigarettes at one of the water stations and getting plenty of takers. I remember costume parties too, and it was usually our leaders who went for broke. We remember Paul in his gorilla costume, flinging dinner rolls across the room; Brad Krause in a perfectly tailored tuxedo and red Converse high-tops; Paul and Natalie as mosquitoes; all of us as fifties' greasers, etc., etc., etc. Don't even get me started on the toga parties.

I remember judging a Kinko's Northwest belching contest at a microbrewery in Portland. The competition was fierce, and the prize money kept growing, until the contest devolved into a food fight and a waitress was hit by flying

E Pluribus Kinko's

pizza. In a moment of indignation and embarrassment, I gave her the prize money, which must have been close to a thousand dollars. If I recall correctly, Brian Wayson was definitely on his way to winning the contest, but "if I recall correctly" is one of the biggest ifs in any history of Kinko's parties.

Stores continuously played pranks and teased one another. For a while there, it was considered bad form if, when calling another store, you did not first pretend to be a customer asking for something absurd, like double-sided transparencies. Considering that I'd actually met a customer who accused our copiers of inserting spelling errors into her documents, I know the coworkers answering the phone had to tread lightly, even when they suspected a prank.

One of the worst equipment mistakes we ever made was the purchase of 150 oversize fax machines. These were fax machines that could transmit a 24 x 36 document. Xerox thought architects and designers would prefer this to Federal Express tubes, but they were wrong. As far as I saw, the primary use of our oversize fax machines was for coworkers to trash-talk one another during sports playoffs. I'm not sure how many millions we spent for the luxury of sending poster-size F-Yous across the country, but it seemed worth it when I saw the coworkers get all fired up to work on their response.

In addition to excessive drinking, romantic hook-ups, food fights, and such, we also tried to keep our business meetings entertaining. At one partner meeting, a group led by Kinko's of Georgia partner Jim Warren performed a skit based on the Joe Isuzu commercials popular at the time. A "customer" walked up to Jim with a giant stack of papers and said, "I made five copies." Jim held up a little sign that said, "She's lying," but charged her for the five copies. The group was promoting copy counter systems to reduce waste/theft in the self-service area. They got a lot of laughs and made their point.

At the 1987 partner meeting in New Orleans, Marketing VP Charley Williams and Kinko's of Oakland partner Dave Faucher performed a blues number about the need for commercial account sales representatives. The lyrics were shoehorned into a "melody," and Dave, at the piano, obviously hadn't slept since he arrived in New Orleans four days earlier. It was hilarious.

Partnership meetings were equal parts fun and work. Executives of Kinko's Northwest used to gather in Maui. We would meet early in the morning, break for a few hours of beach fun, then meet again in the late afternoon, gather for dinner and lighter business, then break again for fun. I'll never forget Mike Fasth standing at a flip chart, trying to concentrate while outside the picture windows behind his audience, whales breached above the bright blue water.

During my Kinko's years, I put on about forty pounds. Anyone traveling three-days-a-week for ten years would likely put on some weight, but part of my gig was wining and dining coworkers. This is hilarious, since I had no social skills: whenever we went out carousing, all I could talk about was work. But when it came to learning and sharing, it sort of worked. I'd get into a town like Seattle or Portland, work in the store for a couple of hours, take some coworkers out to lunch, work in another store for a few hours, take some coworkers out to dinner, visit another store or two, take some coworkers out for drinks, etc. We ate,

E Pluribus Kinko's

drank, and told stories, having fun and building culture. This was how I spread best practices I'd witnessed in other parts of the country.

Our leaders were not just participants in the fun; they were initiators. Promotional videos for the Picnic featured Paul playing guitar with his tongue, or Dan delivering something like beat poetry from the driver's seat of Charley Williams' 1957 Ford Thunderbird convertible. Dan fronted a rock band at many a Picnic, and Paul haunted the hospitality suite, eager to ensure that everyone was having a good time. Out in the field, Paul loved to play off-the-wall games—*Let's all drink Big Gulps and see who can go the longest without having to pee.* Coworkers thought, "This guy's a freak," but they meant it as a compliment. And remember, the first competency of leadership is managing attention.

"Okay," you say, "every company has parties and class clowns. And drinking to excess is hardly a key success factor." True, but remember, the point here is balance and we were balancing a particularly heavy candor. Every company has people who fight and argue and backstab and lie and cheat to get their way, too. We wanted a safe environment for open communication, honest and passionate disagreement, and *forgiveness*.

People subjected to outbursts of Paul's legendary temper would always hear from him soon afterward, when he would earnestly ask, "Are we okay?" Whatever had inspired his outburst was important to him, but so was the relationship. And that's why playfulness was so important at Kinko's: we had to protect the relationships to ensure the candor.

"...But Now You Stop and Think About Your Dignity"

Our many gatherings required coworkers to develop public speaking and presentation skills. Some presenters had better stage presence than others, but everyone seemed to enjoy trying. *Until the rollup.* That's when Joe Hardin, a former Sam's Club executive and the new President of Kinko's, changed the tone, at least in my view. A sales meeting in Las Vegas opened with a Blues Brothers' themed dance number, and Joe gamely jumped around the stage in his dark suit, dark glasses, and stingy-brim fedora. After the number, however, he stood at the microphone and, gasping for breath, said, "See, now you know that I'll do anything to improve sales."

I remember turning to my friend Jim Downey and asking, "Did we just get flipped the bird?" Joe's opening remarks defended his dignity at his audience's expense—we were made to feel guilty for enjoying it. Joe felt he was demeaning himself because we were not meeting sales expectations.

Joe had told me of antics at Sam's Club, like pretending his microphone didn't work at a big meeting where he had to report bad numbers. But again, those were antics in defense of his dignity. Relationships were not as important to our new leaders because their power derived from hierarchy, not a meritocracy of ideas. The rabble was to be exploited, not encouraged. The last thing they wanted was to stir the pot. Instead, they put a lid on it.

Engagement through antagonism felt very natural to me. When hosting a party at our house in the 1960s, my mother would go from room-to-room, making offhand comments about Robert Kennedy, Martin Luther King, Jr., or George Wallace until an argument ensued. Then, extremely pleased with herself, she would move on to the next room to repeat the process until everyone at the party was "participating." At the end of the evening, everyone left with food and hugs and a feeling that *something had happened*. That's how pot stirring worked at Kinko's, too. We instigated zestful controversies and—win or lose—looked forward to the next one. But our memories of personal offense (perceived or real) were subjugated, not erased. And they came back to bite us. Hard.

EPILOGUE: BOY GETS DUMPED

Those Who Learn from the Past

The Coworker's Voice

When I started as front counter copy dude in Eugene ('89), it was typical that many people were early for their shifts. Thirty minutes early was common, sixty minutes was not unheard of. We weren't "allowed" to work, what with labor laws and not being paid and all. So people would sort of hang around in the break room, talking and doing useful chores (counting down tills, cleaning, etc) or hang around in the lobby and help customers with issues on copiers. Not surprisingly, people stayed late as well. When I worked graveyard, the swing shift staff (off at ten to elevenish) typically did not leave until midnight or 1:00 a.m. It was fun to be there.

I probably don't have to spell this out, but this was COLLEGE. There were a million fun places to be and drinking to be done. Yet a group of kids in their early twenties were working our collective asses off at a JOB. Attendance and turnover were rarely an issue.

E Pluribus Kinko's

I challenge anyone to find a retail establishment where that's the case today.

Carl Moyer, Manager, Tukwila, Washington

In the classic Rod Serling short story and *Twilight Zone* episode, "The Monsters are Due on Maple Street," invading extra-terrestrials cause minor disruptions to a neighborhood's electricity, and then sit back to watch as paranoid Earthlings destroy one another. This is pretty much what happened at Kinko's.

In the late 1990s, Kinko's worked with Wall Street heavyweights Goldman Sachs and Clayton, Dubilier and Rice to roll the separate partnerships into a single company, preparatory to going public. In the "new" company, disruptions in the culture turned coworker against coworker. Nothing worked out quite as we hoped, and by the new millennium, nearly all of the founding partners were out of the company, which did not go public and was later sold to FedEx.

The word "nostalgia" comes from the Greek words for home and pain. More or less, nostalgia means the pain of going home. I thought of this as Paul and I spoke to a journalist in 2008 about his perception that Kinko's customer service had declined since the FedEx acquisition. We could not comment directly on the subject, because neither of us has set foot in a Kinko's store for a very long time.

Meeting and exceeding customer expectations had always been a challenge. Now that FedEx has written down nearly the entire purchase price of Kinko's, it's easy to call the acquisition a failure, but is that correct? The rate of technological change was so fast in the late 1990s; we might have failed on our own—with or without the rollup. Or, with 1,000 R&D labs, we might have found a better solution. No one can say for sure, although many offer boastful descriptions of parallel universes. Whatever.

The journalist interviewing us did not seem to understand that FedEx, Kinko's, and Clayton, Dubilier and Rice carried significant cultural baggage into their relationships, and understanding other people's culture is no small task. For example, business people who adhere to the command/control style of management cannot imagine why one would go to the trouble of measuring something and NOT use the results for punitive purposes. Kinko's Service Quality Measurement Program serves as a useful metaphor for everything that went wrong at the end.

Kinko's early reputation for customer service was largely related to speed. As late as the early 1990s, some people were still using thermal paper copiers, but even small xerographic copiers were agonizingly slow. Remember how the entire top section of some models would leisurely slide from side-to-side, rescanning the original once for each copy produced?

When people came to Kinko's for what they considered a big job, say a hundred copies, and the copies were finished within two minutes and looked better than the original (which was often typed with an old ribbon or produced on a dot-matrix printer), it wowed the customer and the

E Pluribus Kinko's

coworker. That shared sense of excitement bonded customer and coworker.

And this bonding occurred between highly educated people with a strong sense of community, too. Until the mid-to-late 1980s, most Kinko's stores were still in college towns and most coworkers were college students or recent graduates. Our busiest stores at that time were serving 300 customers a day and orders of more than 1,000 copies were rare. The entire range of services was pretty much copying, binding, and passport photos.

By the mid 1990s, we had expanded beyond campus communities; the busiest stores were serving more than 1,000 customers per day; overnight orders of 100,000 copies or 5,000 booklets bound with fancy covers were not uncommon. In fact, one of our Los Angeles stores turned around an order for 2.6 million copies in one week!

We were still faster than any alternative, but it didn't *feel* fast, because expectations had risen faster than our systems had advanced. Moreover, the complexity of the jobs increased with the addition of services, like perfect binding, graphic design, custom printing, cutting, folding, computer services, etc. People wanted 11x17 maps folded and bound into a letter-sized document, or covers with gold foil stamping.

With that complexity came many more opportunities for failure. One of our policies was "done right or done over." By the late 1990s, some of my friends in Seattle referred to this policy as "done six times or done seven times," because we learned that, if you serve enough customers, you will meet a surprising number of people who cannot be satisfied.

But we also learned that our machines and our coworkers were imperfect. Under a lot of stress, we made plenty of honest-to-goodness mistakes.

Customer loyalty is the key to profitability for a business with a nickel product, so we focused our training and management programs on the delivery of exceptional customer service. We wanted to reduce errors, but we also wanted to recover from inevitable mistakes. The customer comment postcard was an early outreach program, and customers were not shy about sharing praise or complaints in this manner. We used business reply mail, so it was expensive, but it was also a gold mine of useful information. Customers told us who was rude and who was heroic, and they gave us many ideas for new products and services—how to organize our paper selection so they could find what they needed at multiple locations, what software should be added to our computers, etc.

Then Todd Ordal and Bill Capsalis at K-Graphics, the Kinko's partnership based in Colorado, developed a Service Quality Measurement (SQM) program. I immediately stole it for Kinko's Northwest. Coworkers in my office would receive a store's order forms every week or so, and then set about calling dozens (or hundreds) of the store's customers to poll them about their experience. On a scale from 1-5, they rated the speed of service, courtesy of coworkers, quality of final product, etc. Then we asked for overall comments and ideas for new products and services.

How we used this information changed when Kinko's consolidated its partnerships into a single company. Previously, Kinko's Northwest viewed SQM as a store improvement program and a source of marketing ideas. Results went to the store manager, who could act on the information immediately. Instead of using the data to compare stores, we offered the information as a means for each store to continuously improve their customer relationships. We uncovered dissatisfied customers and re-won their allegiance. We learned which of our services were unknown or misunderstood. We discovered which coworkers should be working with machines rather than with customers. The partnership office conducted Service Quality Measurement as a *service* to the stores.

But after the corporate rollup, SQM scores became part of a national ranking system for stores and managers. The objective was not continuous improvement at the store level, but the use of public praise and humiliation to intimidate managers and exert central authority. The score became more important than the information. Before the rollup, SQM was a joint problem-solving exercise between store management and the home office. After the rollup, SQM was an expensive, labor-intensive rating system that allowed Aeron-chair-bound executives in Ventura to demand the firing of people they'd never met in stores they'd never visited. They turned the program into a pogrom.

Initially, SQM defined store-by-store benchmarks and provided timely information to managers, who could act instantly to resolve issues. Each store competed against itself, to improve scores by providing better service. Our goal was to furnish useful information to the manager. After the rollup, SQM became part of a nationwide competition with dire consequences for those in the bottom quartiles. Sure, we had stack-ranked stores before the rollup, but not for institutionalized punishment.

As bossiopaths assumed power in the new company, they may have actually believed that improved customer service would result from punishing and humiliating stores with low SQM scores. Naturally, this led some stores to game the system, because as any experienced manager will tell you: you get what you measure. Originally, we measured the quality of customer service. After the rollup, SQM measured the managers' fear of punishment and humiliation.

Which brings me back to cultural conflict. The new corporate masters at Kinko's were simply seeking a more efficient way to manage (read: control) a far-flung empire. Such people cannot appreciate the difference between efficiency and effectiveness. Before the rollup, we did a lot of very inefficient things to keep our coworkers engaged and excited. So-called executives like myself spent most of our time in the stores, listening to coworkers and customers. Dozens of full-time coworkers devoted each day to interviewing customers. We had a good reputation for customer service AND we were making plenty of money. Could it be that efficiency is a false idol? I think so, but if you go around tearing down the new culture's idols, don't be surprised to find yourself exiled.

I was neither a partner nor a particularly important coworker at the time of the corporate rollup, but I expressed my opposition to Paul. Too many people, both newcomers and veterans, declared that Kinko's would have to behave more like other companies in order to go public. But

E Pluribus Kinko's

marketing people are obsessed with uniqueness, so that sounded like a death knell to me.

But, for a lot of good reasons (and a few I don't like), the partnerships did rollup into a single company, and the transition period was stressful for everyone. I was nearly manic with anger. One day, fellow veteran Kathy Huff and I were walking up Oak Street in downtown Ventura. As we approached Main Street, the crowd thickened. Kathy stopped me and we stood on the sidewalk, people-watching for a minute or two. Then she pointed out that none of those people gave a damn about what was going on at Kinko's and they seemed to be much happier than I was. I couldn't argue.

Soon afterwards, many of my old friends were gone, and I was ashamed that—blinded by dreams of an IPO and remembrance of historical grievances—the rest of us had abandoned one another during the new management's purges of our coworkers. At the risk of trivializing the historical reference, I used to paraphrase Pastor Martin Niemöller's poem about the Nazi's systematic removal of their targets: When they came for Sales VP Greg Soulages, I did not speak up, because I was not Greg Soulages, and I had issues with his sales department anyway. When they came for Marketing VP Karen Sophiea, I did not speak up, because I was not Karen Sophiea, and I had issues with her marketing department anyway. When they came for Mike Fasth and Brad Krause and Dan Frederickson, I did not speak up for some petty reason. Naturally, when they came for me, there was no one left to speak up.

A bit melodramatic, I know, but it's a shameful memory, since I have always maintained that Kinko's ultimate competitive advantage was the fact that every coworker had a voice.

The Coworker's Voice

In November 2001 I drove from my home in Champaign to the "career counseling" session in Chicago that was part of my severance package from Kinko's, Inc. After an eighteen-year run with Kinko's, from campus store manager to Regional Manager to post rollup Divisional Training Director to some sort of Director of Training Implementation, I was one of the last to go when Kinko's, Inc., dismantled its field training organization.

I completed the job skills questionnaires and evaluations and met with my advisor. His comment to me, after reviewing the material, was something to the effect of, "How were you ever successful and satisfied with these jobs, with this company? You don't test out well for these jobs at all." "Exactly!" was my reaction. That comment to me was one of the most telling about the kind of company Kinko's really was. It was a place for a wide variety of geeks and artists, jocks and hippies, misfits and characters that didn't fit the mold of traditional business people, and we were successful, not in spite of it, but because of it.

Jim Downey, Regional Manager, Kinko's Graphics Corporation

What Makes You So Special?

When I take on a new marketing assignment, I spend a lot of time interviewing the company's coworkers and executives, pressing this simple question: "What makes you so special?" I also interview customers.

Too many executives delude themselves, believing that vague notions of excellent value or product quality make their offering unique, but this is almost never true. If your business is unique, it's because of something very specific and identifiable. If your business is not unique, you are living on borrowed time. (By the way, executives are notoriously susceptible to their own internal PR campaigns. When they start blathering away about "integrity," I know I should demand my fee in advance. People with integrity don't have to talk about it. Their customers handle that chore.)

I drive two concepts home during this interview process: 1) "Unique" means more than uncommon—to be unique is to be the ONE AND ONLY. 2) Only the customer can see your company objectively. If you don't listen to customers

E Pluribus Kinko's

every single day, you don't know what's special about your product or service. And if you don't know what's special about your business, you risk losing it.

The greatest irony of Kinko's decision to roll its 126 partnerships into a single company was that those who criticized the call to unify were branded as "resistant to change." Well, we'd been "eating change for breakfast," to borrow an expression from Tom Peters, but not all change is progress.

I have to admit that the new owners clearly embraced change on a scale we had not imagined—in just the six years following the rollup, Kinko's changed its top executives repeatedly. Presidents or CEOs included Don Gogel, Joe Hardin, George Tamke, Gary Kusin, Ken May, and Brian Phillips. Chief Financial Officers included Bennett Nussbaum, Jeff Moxie, Bill Benac, Mark Blinn, and Leslie Benners. Chief Information Officers included Bob Meltzer, Fred Herczeg, Allen Dickason, Dan Conners, Laurie Zeitlin, and Richard Maranville. The new owners apparently ate change for breakfast, lunch, and dinner, but I'm not sure how well it agreed with them.

I can't tell you how many consultants and paratrooper executives (those that seemed to drop into the company out of nowhere) told me it was time for Kinko's to "grow up and be more like other companies." That advice must top the chart of history's most dubious business recommendations.

It is absolutely true that a unique company cannot stay the same as it grows, but it must strive to stay unique. Otherwise, the leadership is willfully choosing to abandon competitive advantage—for coworkers and customers—and accelerate the decline stage of the profit life cycle. Of course, the company must KNOW what makes it unique.

Kinko's independent partnership structure encouraged and rewarded agility and experimentation, and kept the company's owners very close to its customers and coworkers. The corporatization of Kinko's solved certain problems—like creating an exit strategy for the largest partners—but stripped the company of its individuality. Maybe this was inevitable with so much growth, but I don't think so, and I urge you, whatever your line of business, to ask this question every day: what makes us so special?

In late summer 1999, after yet another reorganization (but far from the last), my new boss wanted to fire me and I wanted to quit, so one Saturday morning in September, I packed up my office, loaded up my car, and drove past the guard gate for the last time, flipping off the security camera for good measure. I took a year off to write screenplays and watch cartoons with my kids. Then I worked at a couple of other Paul Orfalea-related companies for a few years, eventually launching Dizzy One Ventures, primarily to write this little book. As Kinko's Regional Manager Jim Downey would say, "Difficult labor, small baby."

But now, ten years after Paul and I left Kinko's, as FedEx removes the brand from the commercial landscape, I think about Kathy Huff's comment and know that, while I couldn't argue that people outside of Kinko's didn't care about what was happening to the company in 1999, *I wasn't one of them and I did care.* And I still do, because, while there are many ways to run a company, Kinko's Philosophy, Partnership Ethos, and Pot-stirring did a lot of good for a

E Pluribus Kinko's

lot of people, and present useful templates for entrepreneurs who want to succeed without sacrificing their democratic sensibilities—who want to enter their houses justified.

The inverse of George Santayana's famous admonition applies here: those who learn from the past are **NOT** condemned to repeat it. Kinko's success diminished in direct proportion to its loss of democracy. Paul used to tell us that he liked our democratic structure because no democracy had ever lost a war. I'm not sure that's strictly true, but I do believe that democracy is always worth fighting for. What do you believe?

Afterword: Brad and Stuie

Brad and Stuie Krause saved my life.

I've mentioned in this manuscript that my two years working with Charley Williams were difficult for me. *Sorry, Charley—I know they weren't pleasant for you, either.* Early in 1988, Charley and I were in Pasadena, California, producing television ads for the annual 2.5¢ Sale. The partner was—justifiably—ripping me a new one every night, because we were trashing her freshly remodeled store and inconveniencing her customers. I was not yet aware of my propensity for low blood sugar or the powerful way it played on my moods. Working twenty-hour days, Charley and I were in a state of continuous creative difference. And we were sharing a hotel room. During a power failure (of course) one morning, I stood in the pitch-black bathroom, holding my razor in front of my half-shaved face, wondering whose throat I should cut.

The night before, back in Santa Barbara, my wife had joined our neighbor, Kit Tryon, and her sister, Stuie Krause, at a UCSB Arts & Lectures musical performance. During

E Pluribus Kinko's

the intermission, Stuie asked my wife how things were going on the commercial shoot. My wife replied, "I haven't heard from Dean, but I haven't heard from the police either, so he and Charley haven't killed each other yet."

I'll never know for sure, but I suspect this is why, after I abandoned Charley at a car rental agency in Pasadena and drove to Santa Barbara to clean out my office and quit my job, I found a note from Brad Krause waiting on my desk. He and Mike Fasth wanted to talk to me about creating a Marketing Manager position at Kinko's Northwest.

Thanks to Brad and Stuie's gentle and generous intervention, I enjoyed a long career at Kinko's Northwest and learned from a team of mentors including Mike Fasth, Steve Williams (Charley's brother!), Tom Parrish, Peggy VanWaard, Ross Waddell, Greg Soulages, John Walker, Lynn Huston, and oh-so-many-more citizen coworkers. I am forever grateful for the experience.

Brad and Stuie were not always my biggest fans, but they appreciated my abilities and I think they believed that people who worked for a second chance should get one. As part of their family, I was able to kick a drug habit, mature as a person, and start my own family.

Brad believed in positive thinking and helped to remove an enormous chip from my shoulder. He taught me, through his own example, that happiness is a choice. I've tried to live up to Brad's patient reminder back when my temper used to get the better of me: "Just try to keep it positive."

We lost Brad to cancer in 2007 and Stuie to an accident in 2009. I hope this book, in its celebration of the culture they helped to create and continuously nurtured, honors their memory.

APPENDIX:

10 Suggestions for a Healthy Commercial Democracy

State Your Values Clearly

The Philosophy empowered new and far-flung coworkers to make good decisions on their own and ensured every coworker a voice in the company. The Philosophy also attracted and encouraged people aligned to the values it described.

Honor Freaks and Curmudgeons

The Philosophy and Commitments to Communication came to life through constant testing; public debates demonstrated our commitment to open communication and our love of diverse ideas. Diversity of ideas is just as valuable as any other kind of workplace diversity.

Don't Bogart Ownership

The unique partnership structure spread opportunity but also burdens. This allowed the company to grow without becoming beholden to an outside entity. Paul said he'd be happier with a smaller piece of a much bigger pie and the pie certainly grew. Moreover, *profit sharing and the democratic culture spread a feeling of ownership—and responsibility—to people who held no equity.*

Centralize Only What MUST be Centralized

Liberty breeds innovation, so try to give remote locations as much liberty as possible. "As the founder and senior partner, I could have dictated anything, but once you start doing that, you demoralize your workforce and end up having to dictate everything. You need people to make good decisions for themselves. You might be able to require white paint and blue counters, but can you dictate a passion for customer service? Your company culture will be determined, to a great extent, by the level of personal trust between you and your coworkers," Paul Orfalea said.

Demand Participation

Everyone hates meetings and newsletters, because most meetings and newsletters suck. But our conclaves, Picnics, company meetings, sales meetings, committees, and other gatherings were reunions that created new opportunities for distant relatives to meet and learn new things from one another. And our newsletter was more like an enthusiast magazine—*Popular Photography* or *Cat Fancy*, with the right blend of gossip, useful information, and amusements.

Gather the Tribe

As much a family reunion as a business meeting, the Picnic built a feeling of unity without demanding conformity. The company thrived on the free flow of ideas, and mass gatherings allowed more people to learn from each other.

Encourage Experimentation by Practicing Forgiveness

Liberty at the partnership level allowed us to try lots of new services and products. The newsletters I've seen from

1983–1986 are full of "try this!" articles, as well as coworkers asking, "How do you handle this?" Some companies need 1,000 cookie cutter stores—every Williams Sonoma store looks and acts exactly the same. Kinko's was based on providing widespread, affordable access to new technologies otherwise too expensive for individuals, so we needed to stay in tune customer-by-customer and feel free to try new things. But this only worked because we also shared failures without fear of recrimination.

Stir the Pot

Kinko's was blessed with a world-class pot-stirrer in Paul Orfalea. He fought complacency but also kept people focused on the Philosophy—and profits! To make the most of a democratic workplace, leadership must keep the environment roiling to promote individual engagement. People arguing passionately achieve more than people sleepwalking.

Play

Don't take yourself too seriously. Once I had seen KGC President Mark Madden wearing a plastic bozo head on the dance floor in an Indianapolis bar, I knew we could talk about anything. Yeah, coworkers played hard, and coworkers fraternized and formed friendships, but guess what? People will do a lot for their friends.

Pursue Profits Unashamedly

Building mutual prosperity into the Philosophy was a brilliant move. Paul was never shy about making money and he always bravely said that happy fingers ring happy cash registers; that Kinko's treated coworkers well because it was good business. Honesty creates respect (not in the dogmatic anti-capitalists, but hey, you can't please everybody) and defines the goals to which we direct our liberty.

Acknowledgements

Writing may be a solitary craft, but creating this book was very much a team effort. I'm grateful for the support and contributions from Paul Orfalea, Dan Frederickson, Mike Fasth, Fred Fleet, Carl Moyer, and all the coworkers who participated online. I especially want to thank Karen Madden, who read multiple versions of the manuscript and—in the best Kinko's style—used the expression "I disagree" often. My wife, Laurie, is an excellent editor and sounding board, but she also had to endure over a decade of me complaining about working at Kinko's and another decade of me complaining about not working at Kinko's. Upon publication of this book, I promise I'll find something else to complain about.

About The Author

As the Managing Partner and "Guerrilla Writer" for Dizzy One Ventures LLC, Dean Zatkowsky co-authors or ghostwrites articles, blogs, screenplays, and books for individuals, businesses, and non-profit organizations. Prior to launching Dizzy One in 2007, Dean served as a Marketing executive for Kinko's (1986-1999), DataProse (2000-2005), and West Coast Asset Management (2005-2007). He is co-author of *The Entrepreneurial Investor: The Art, Science and Business of Value Investing* (Wiley, 2007) and *Two Billion Dollars in Nickels: Reflections on the Entrepreneurial Life* (BookSurge, 2008).

www.ingramcontent.com/pod-product-compliance
Lightning Source LLC
Chambersburg PA
CBHW071413170526
45165CB00001B/267